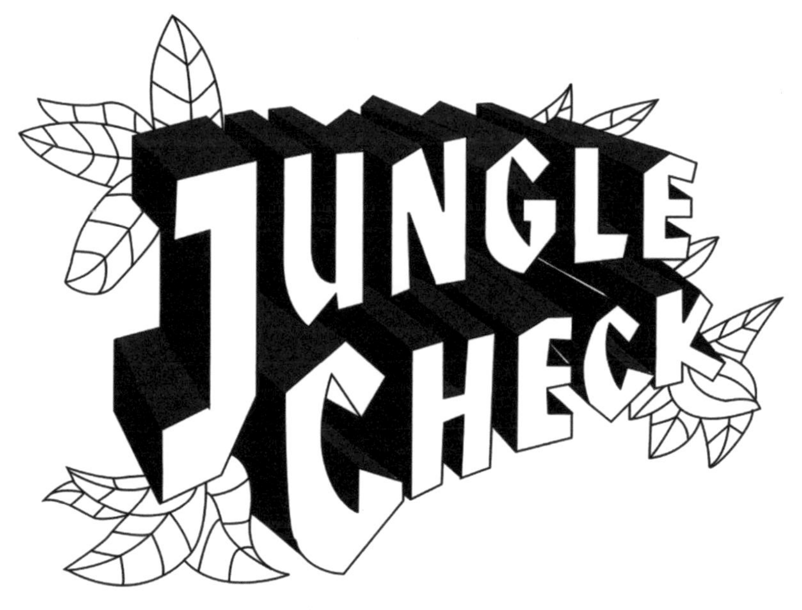

CRISTINA DE MIDDEL & KALEV ERICKSON

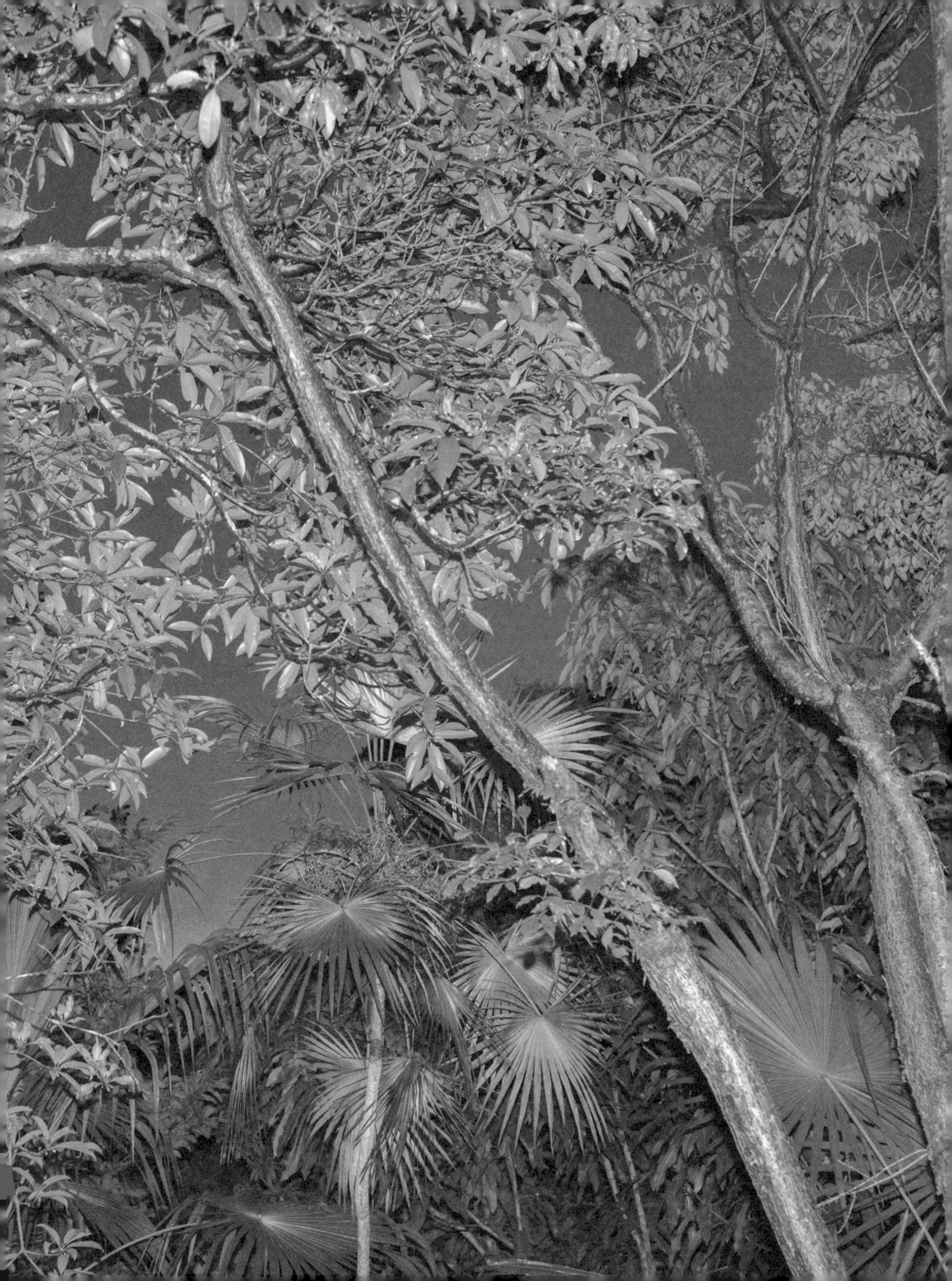

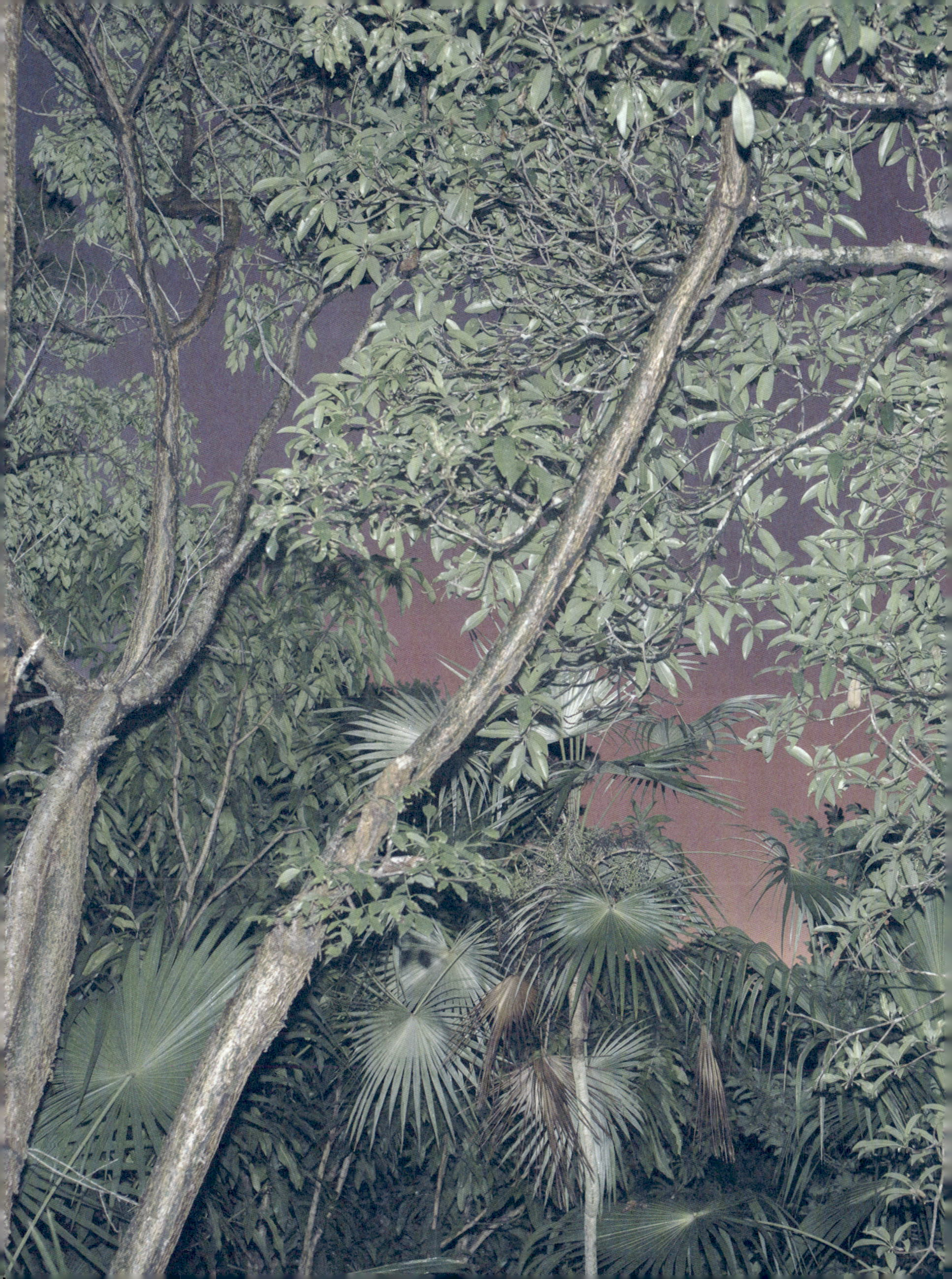

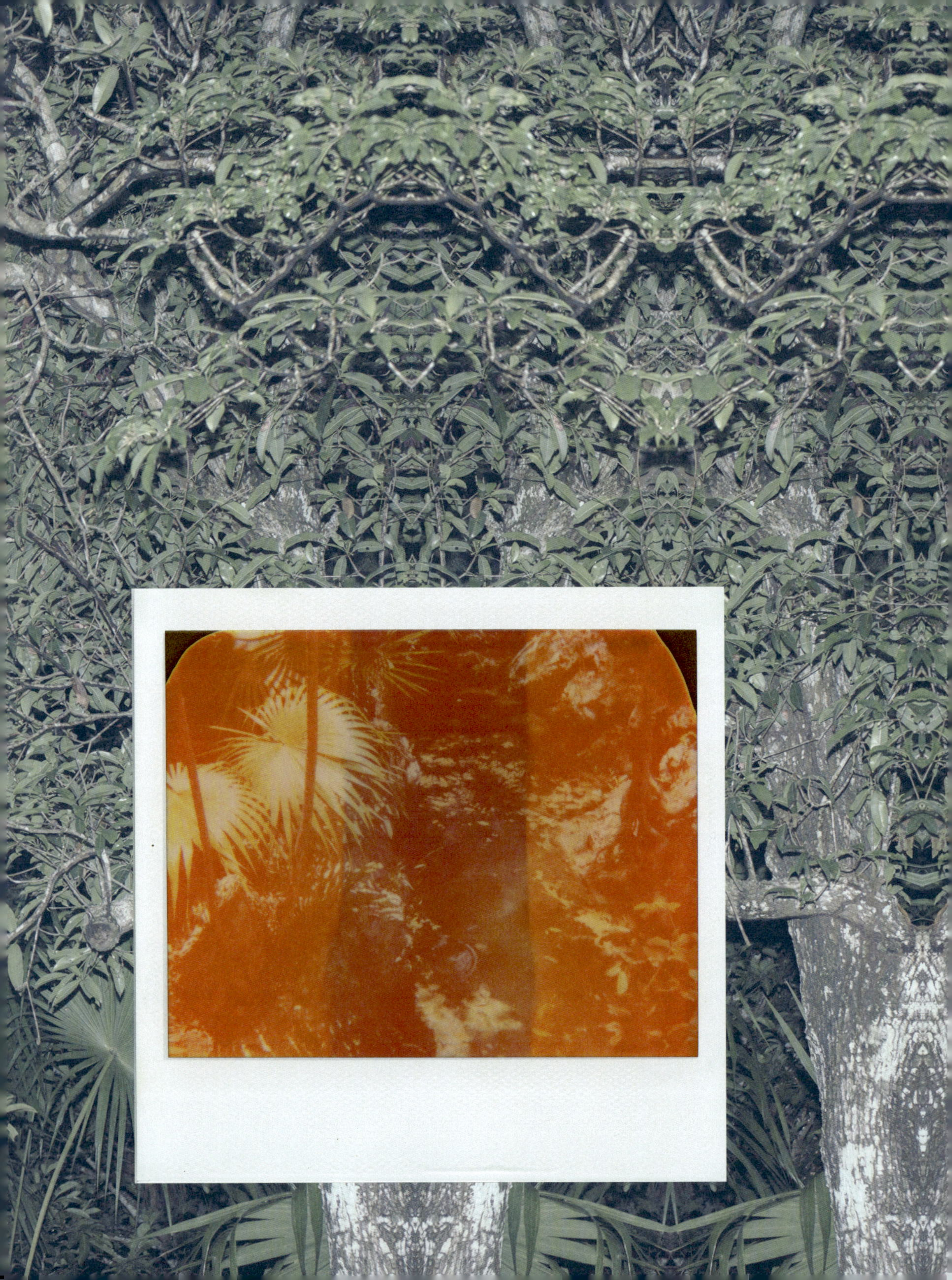

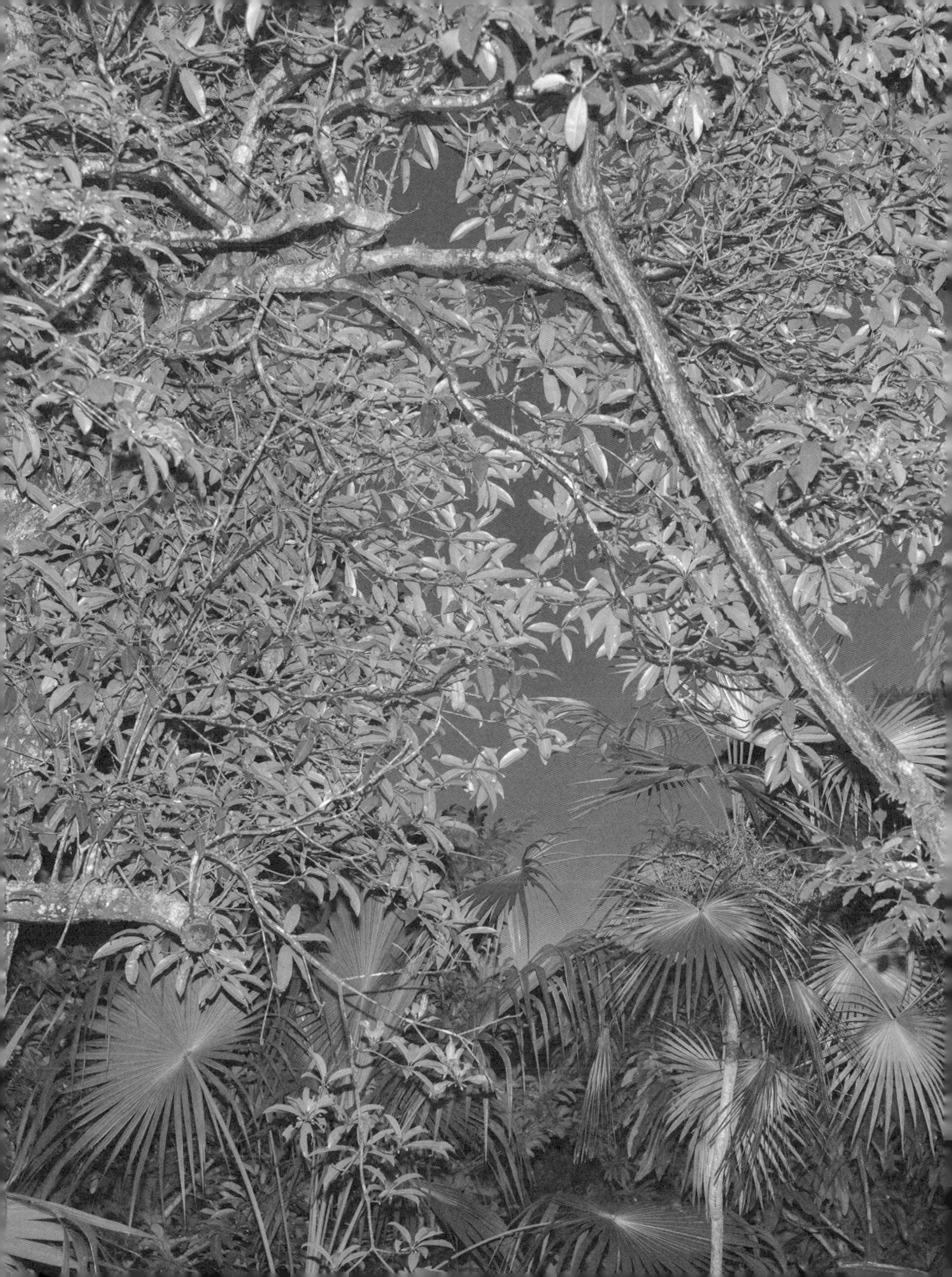

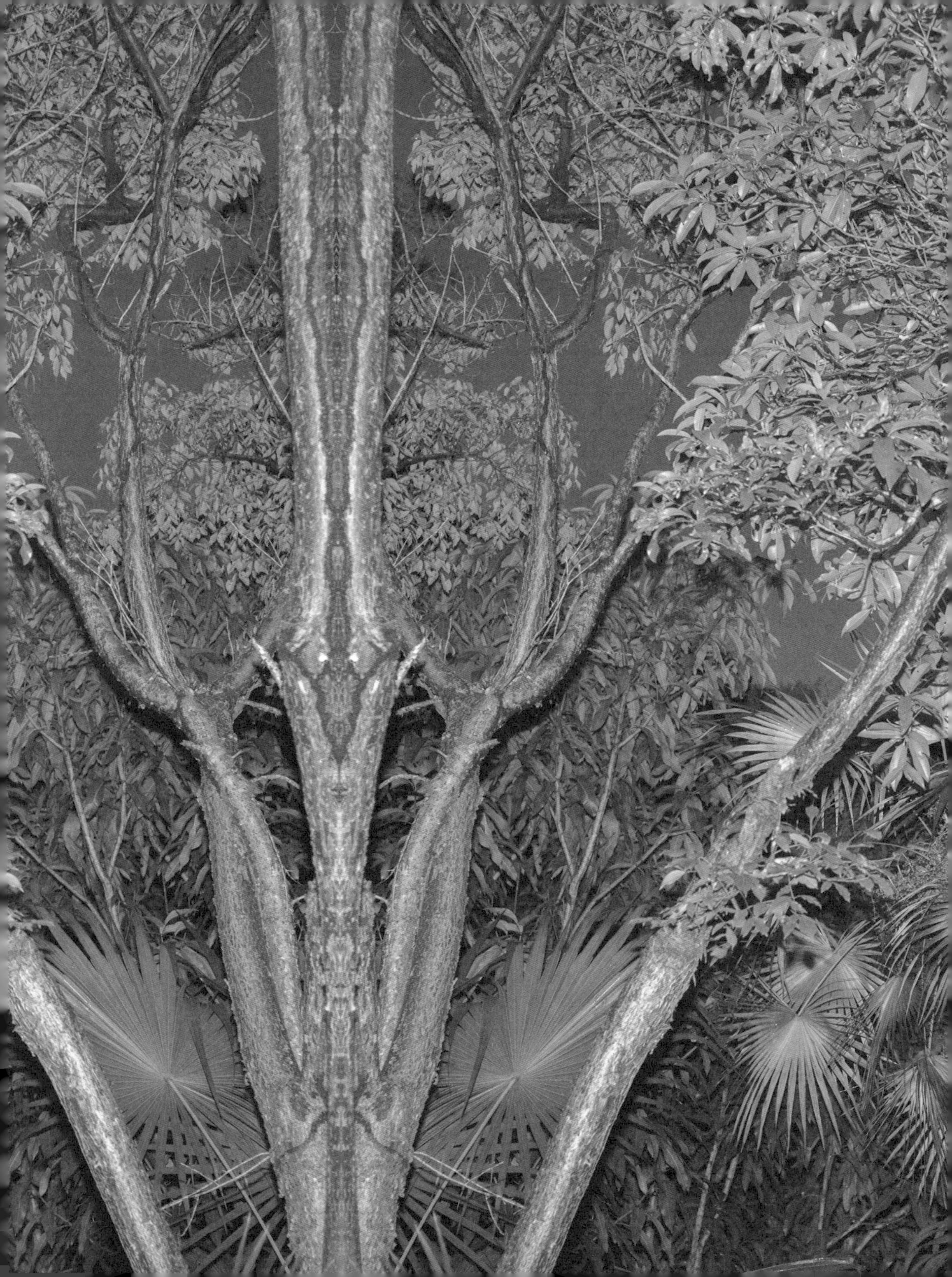

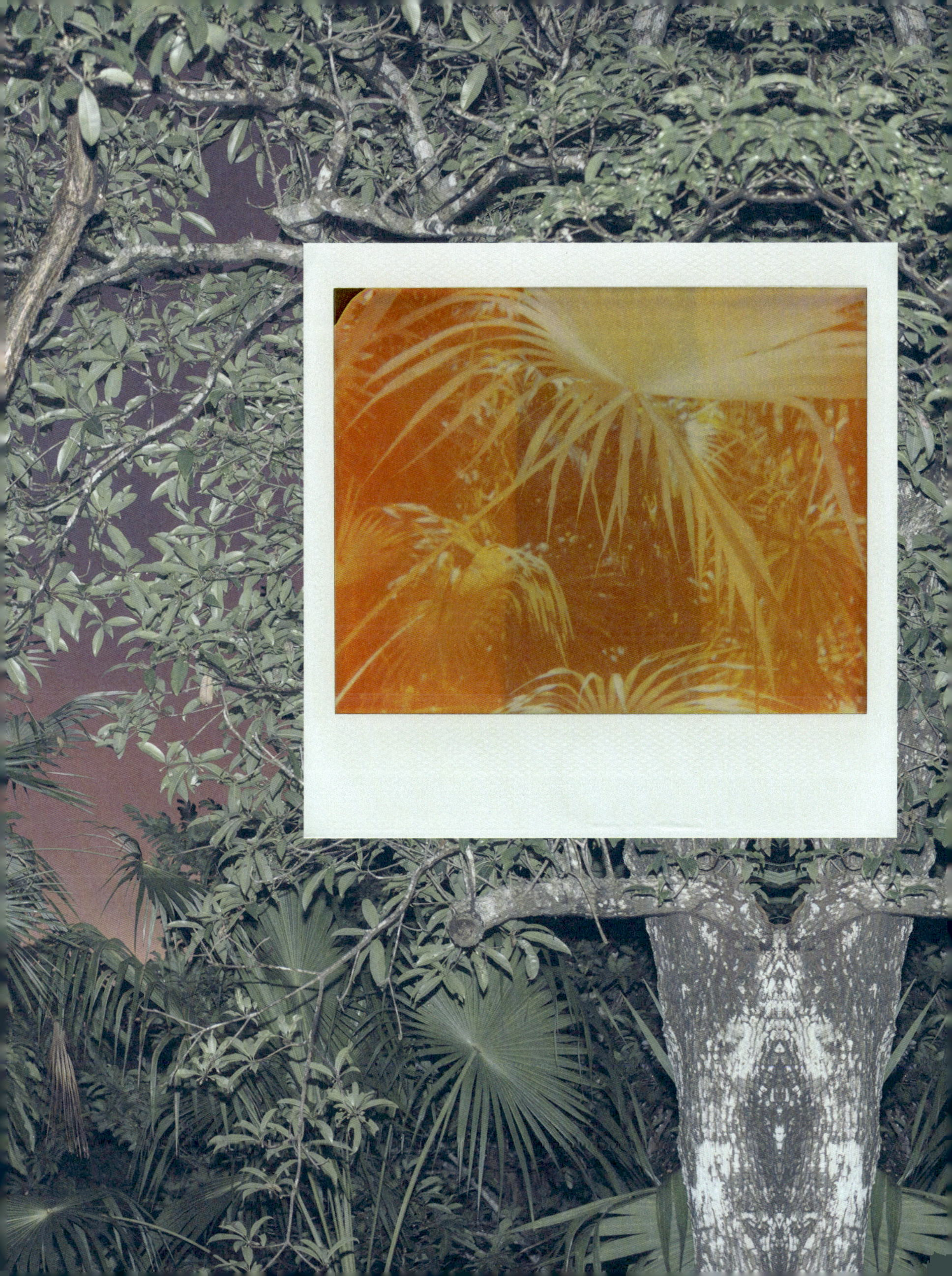

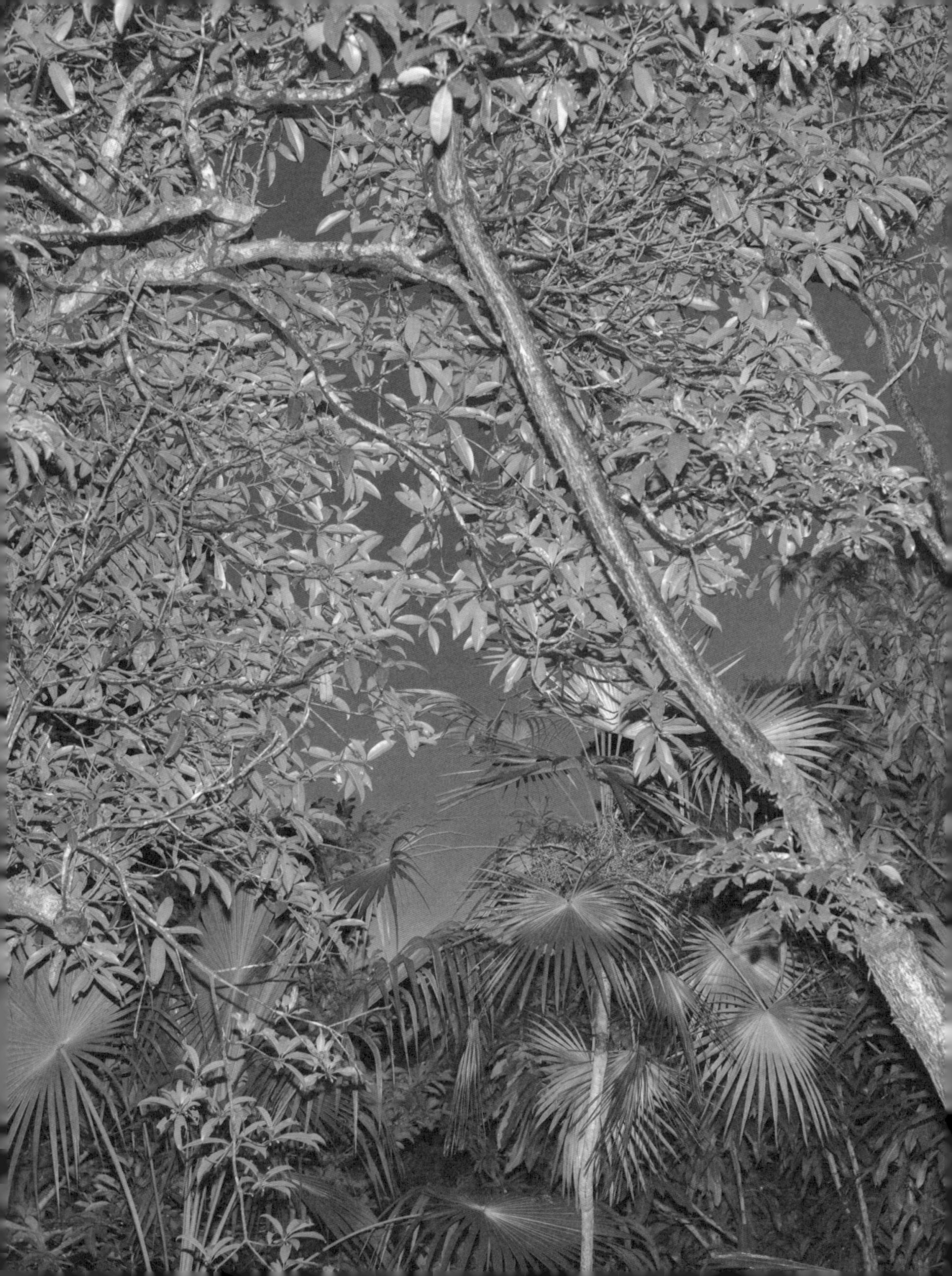

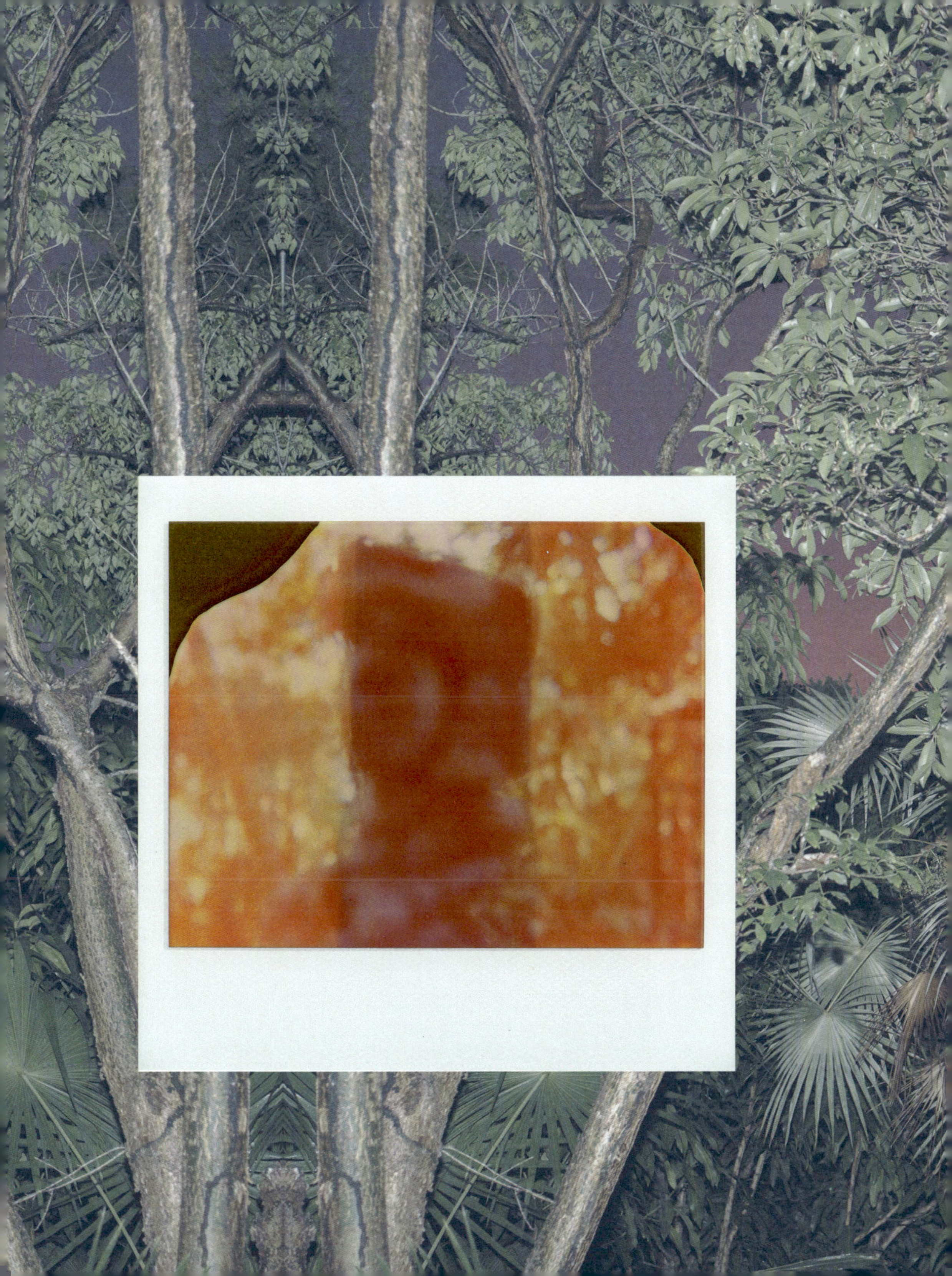

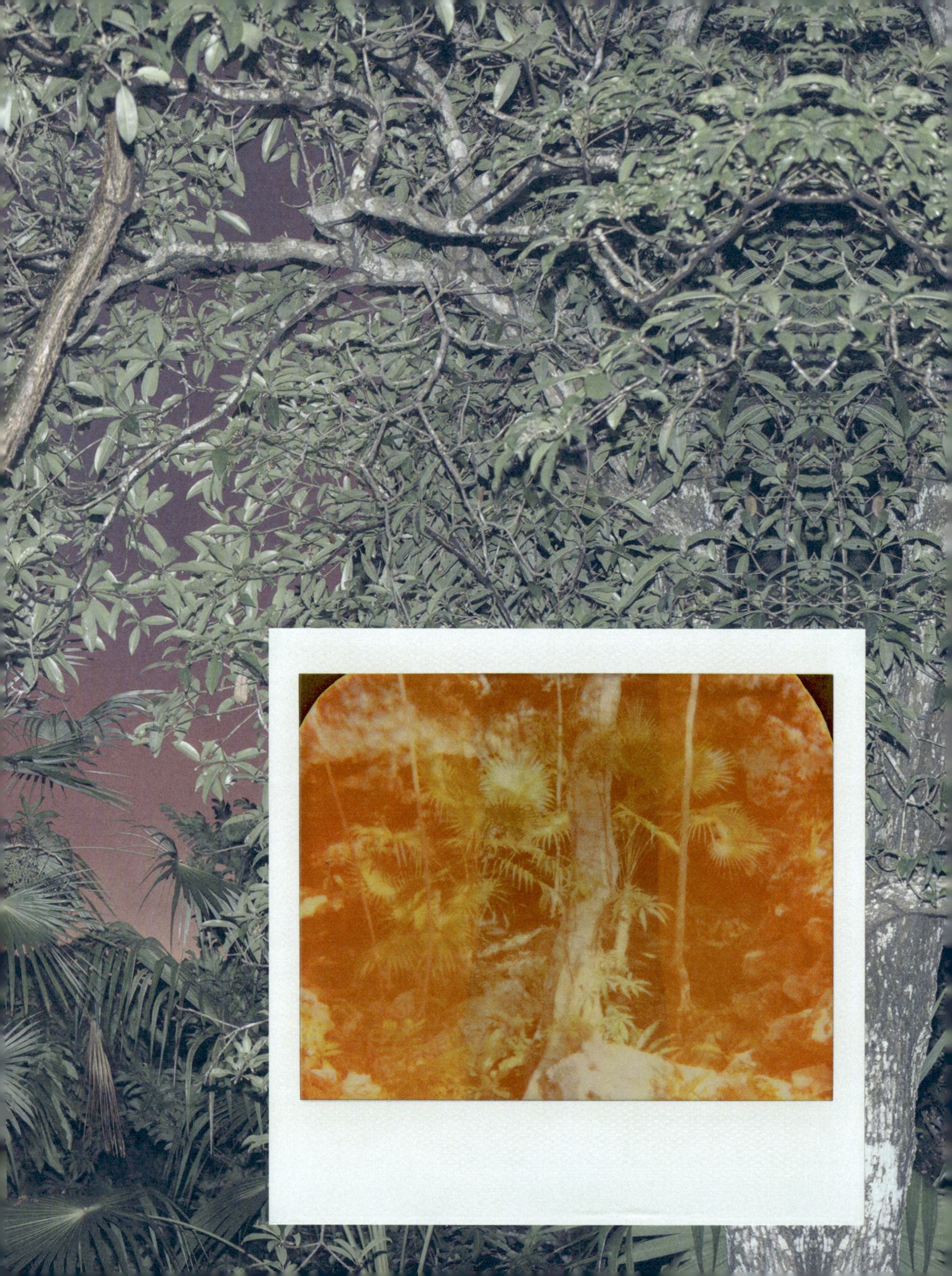

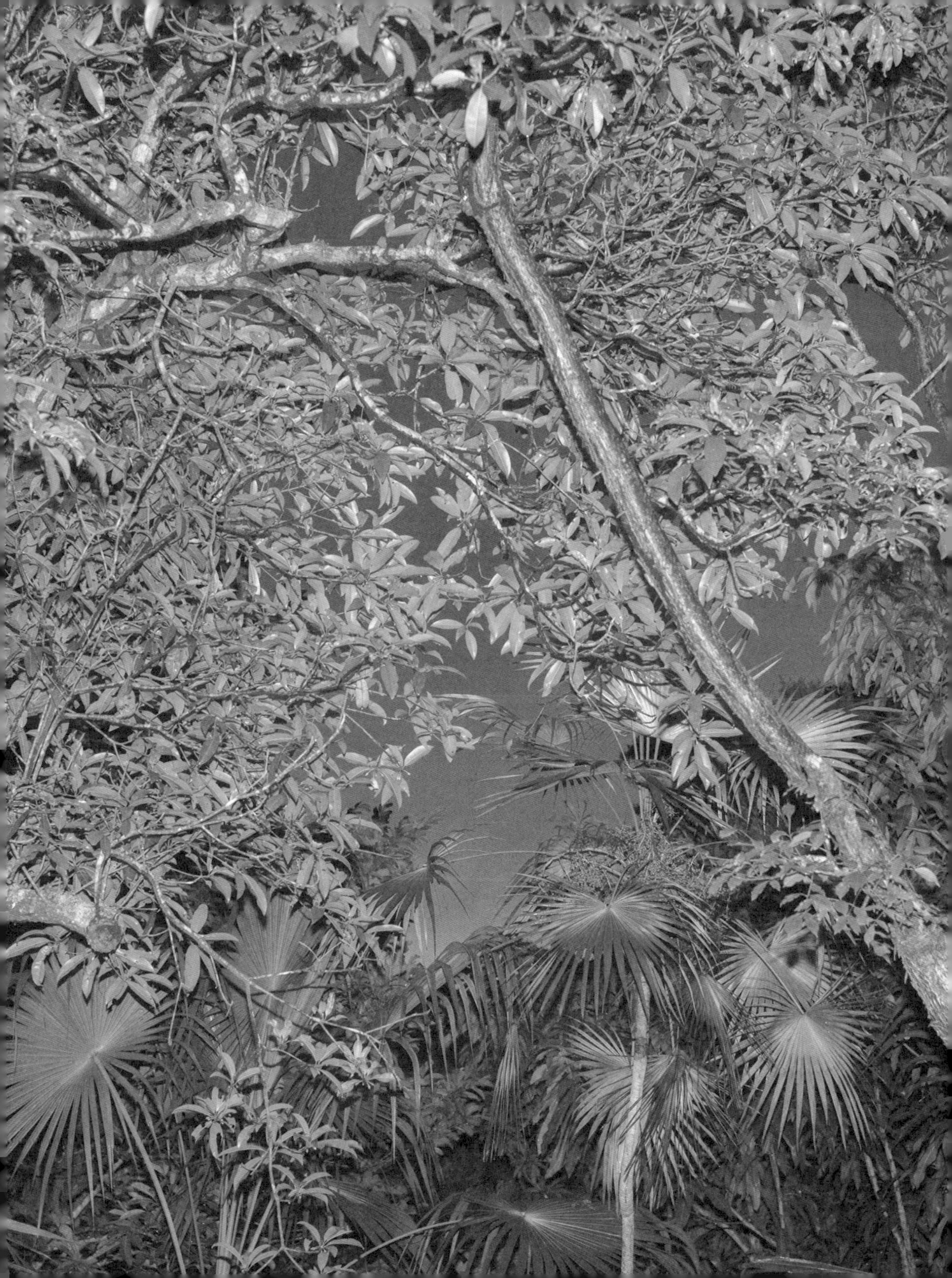

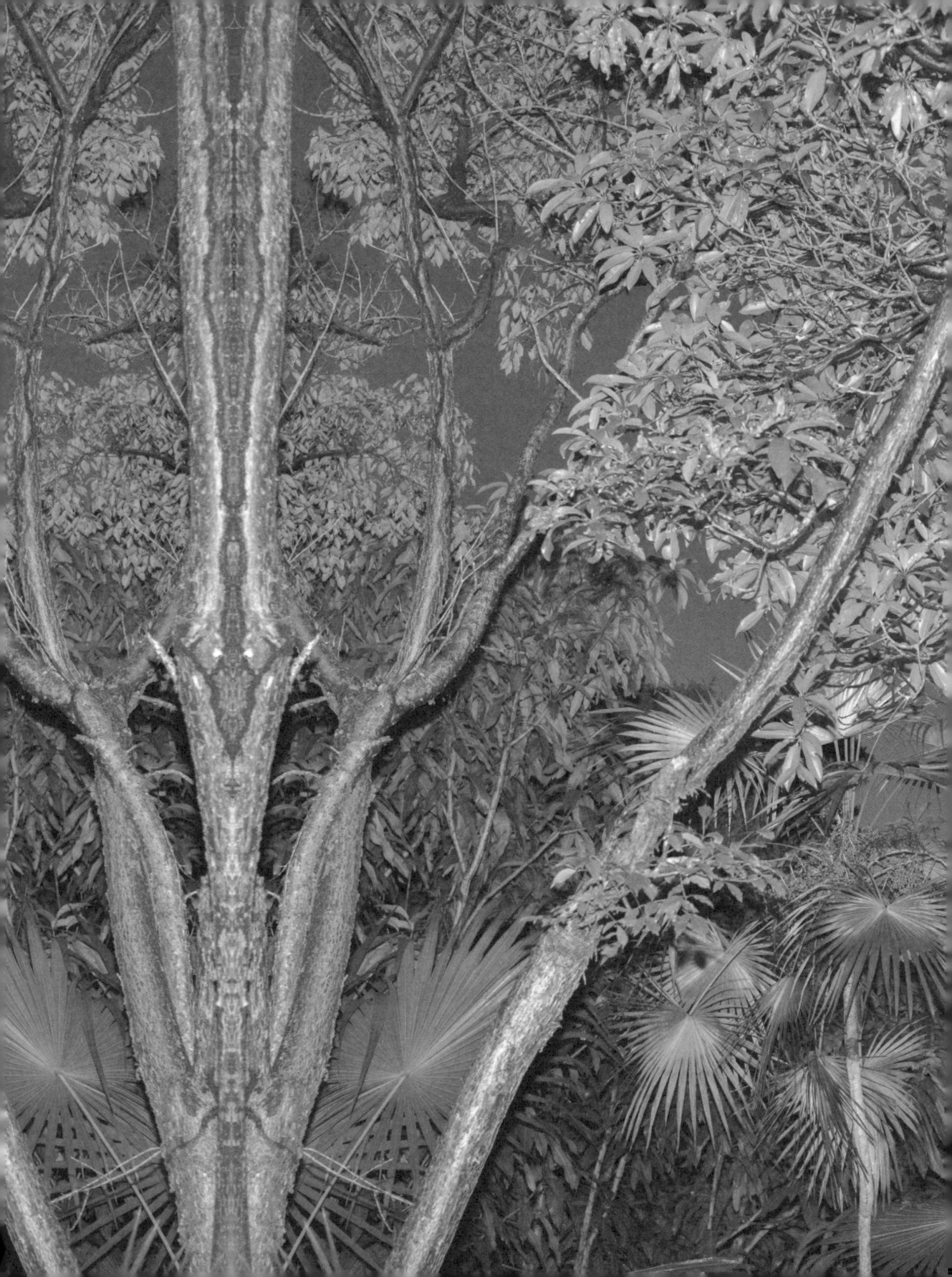

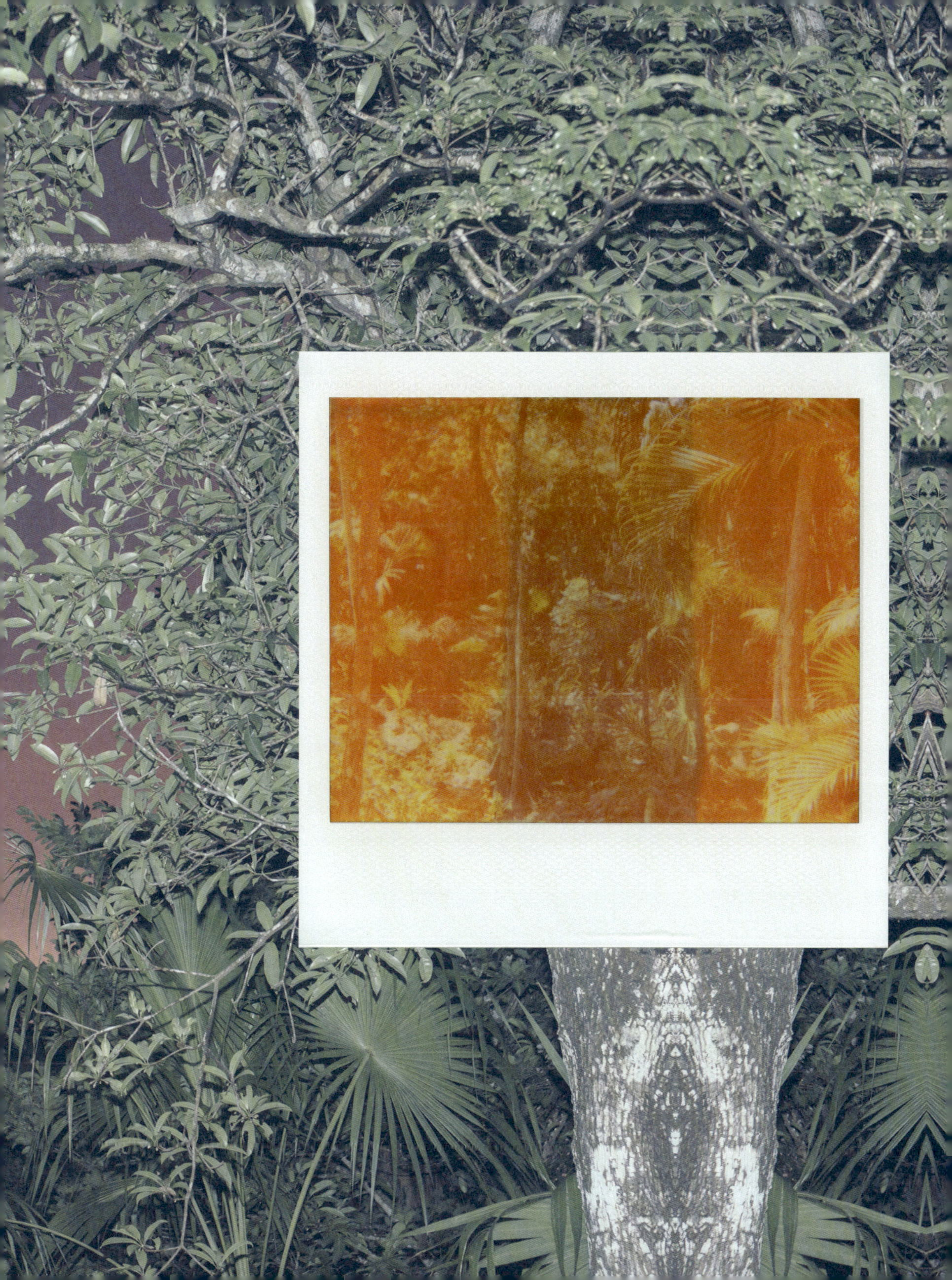

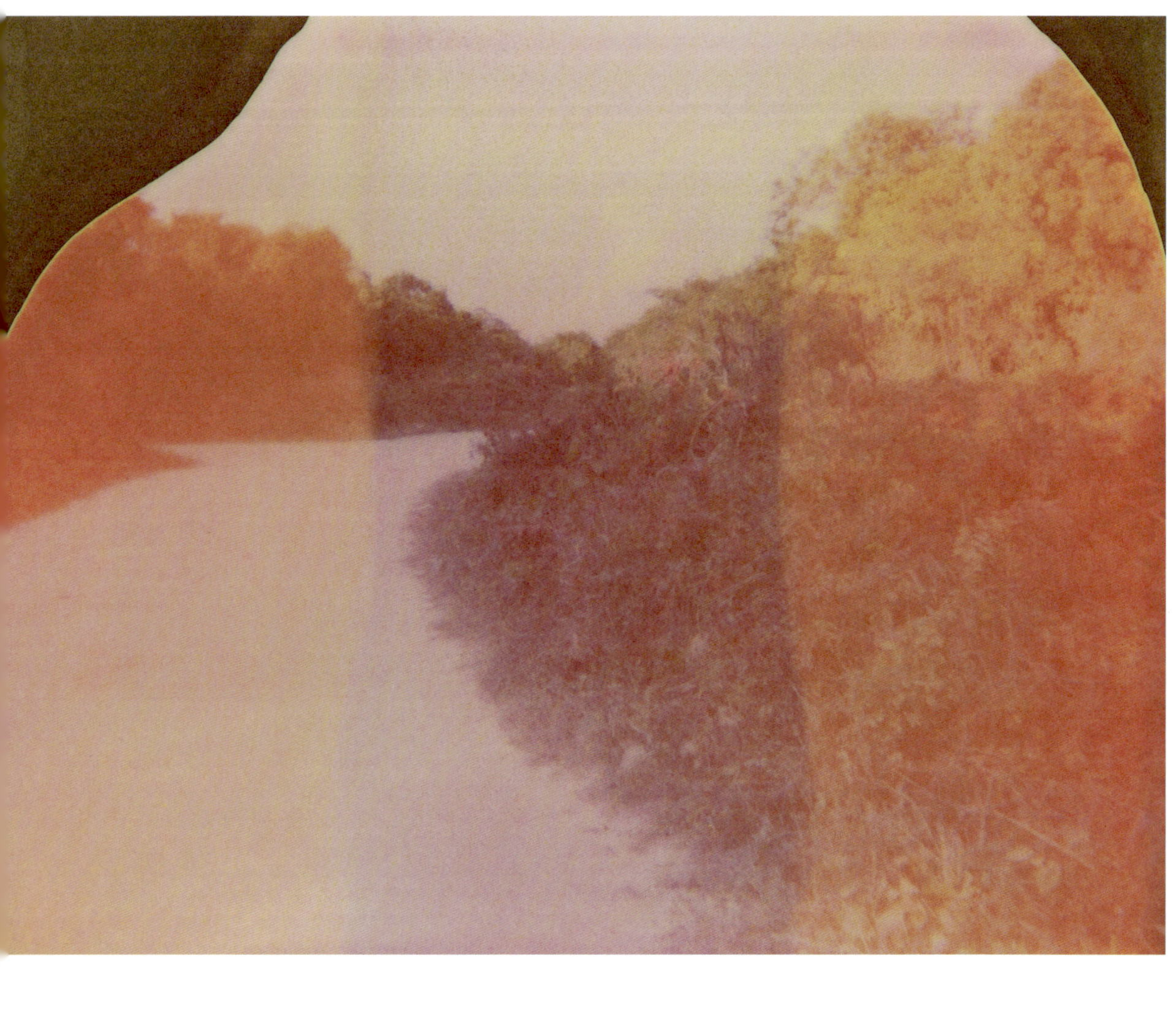

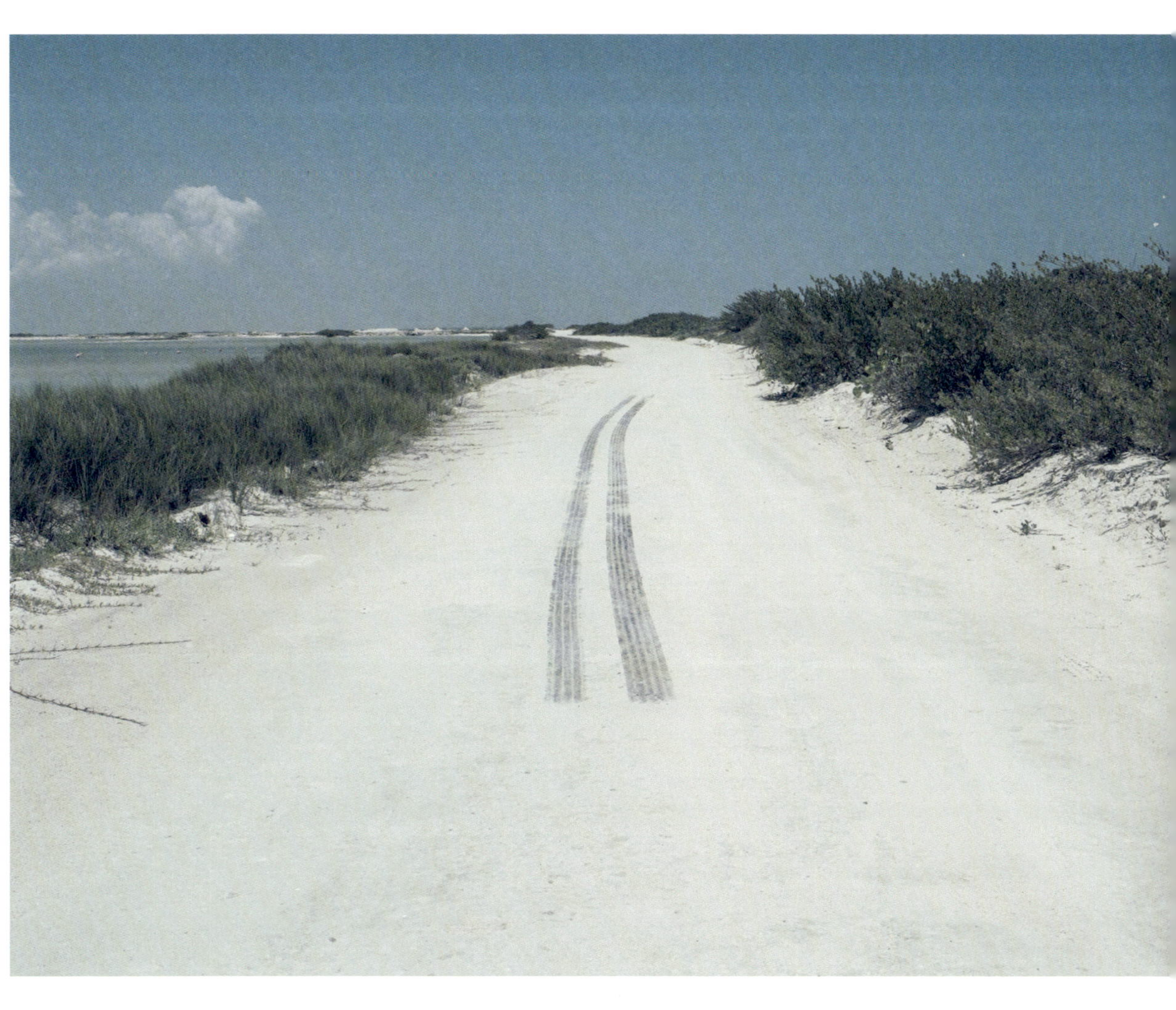

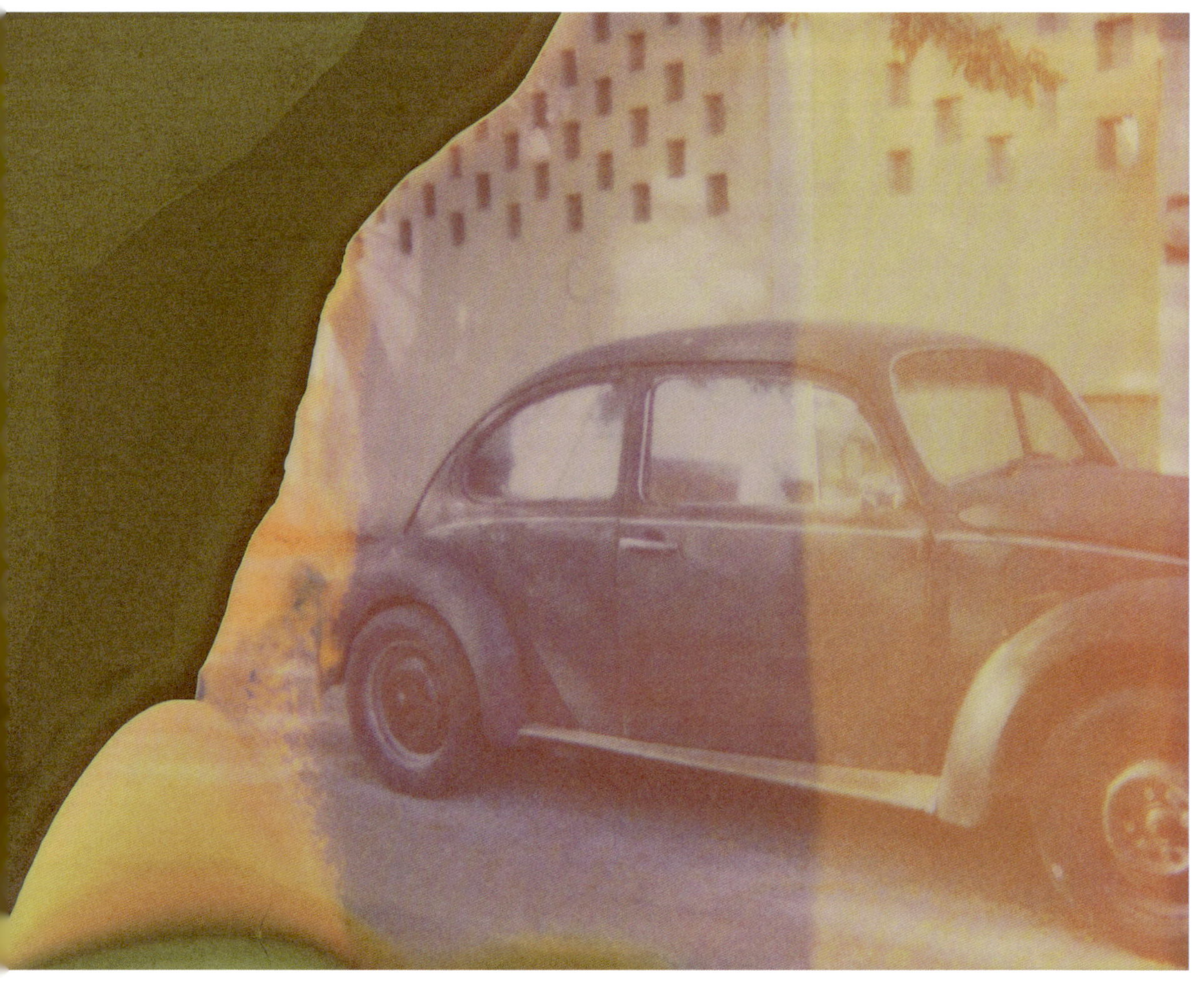

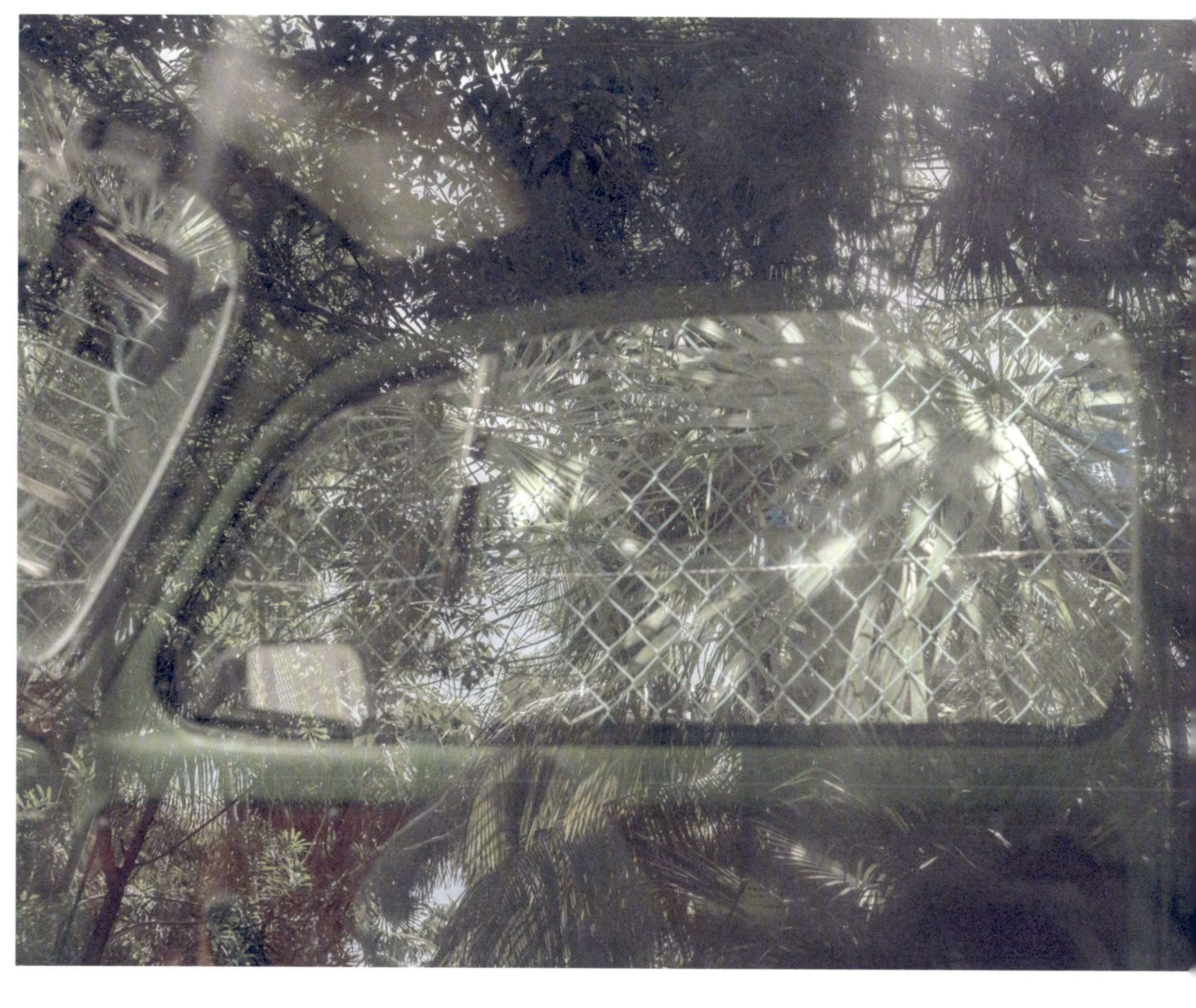

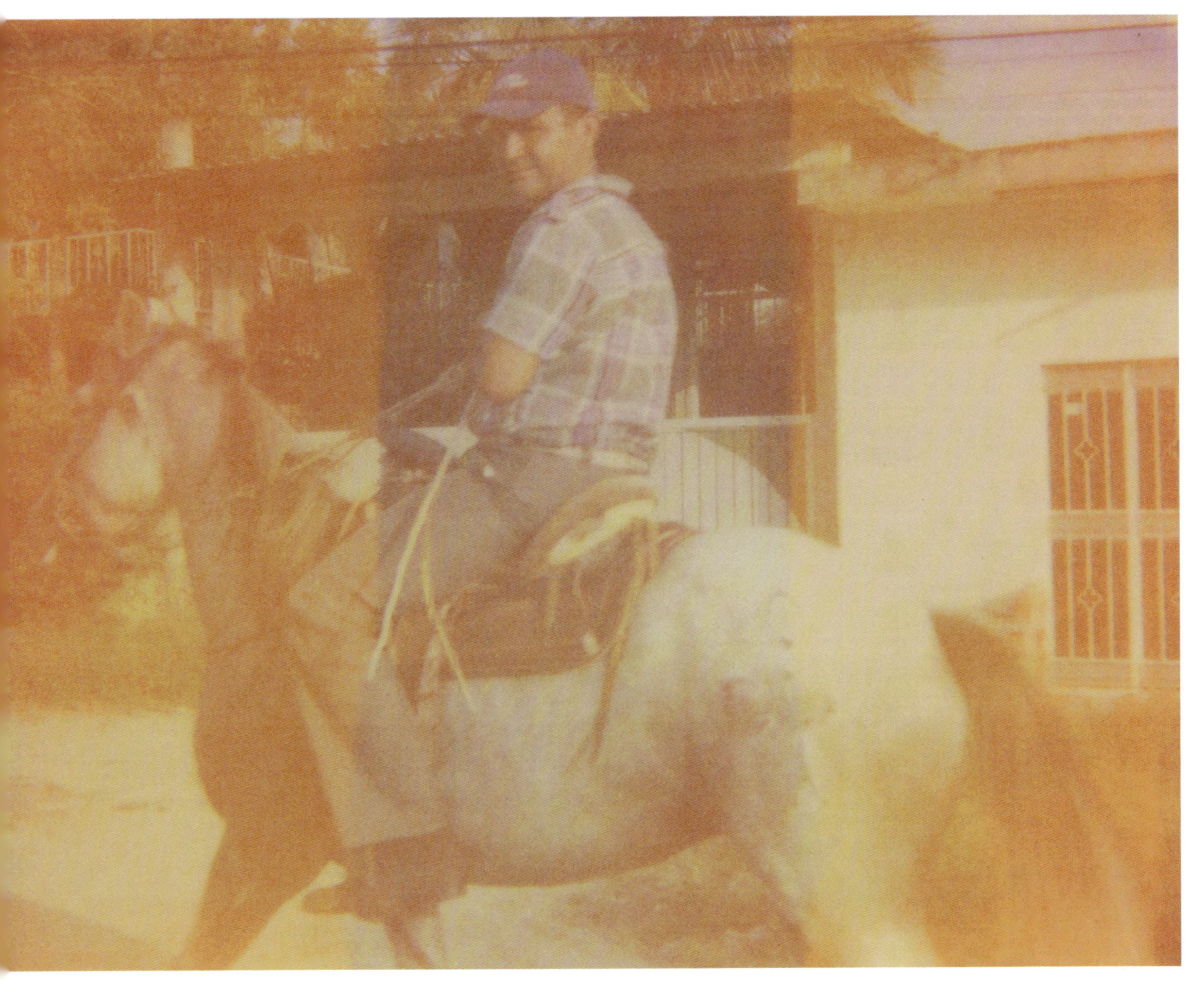

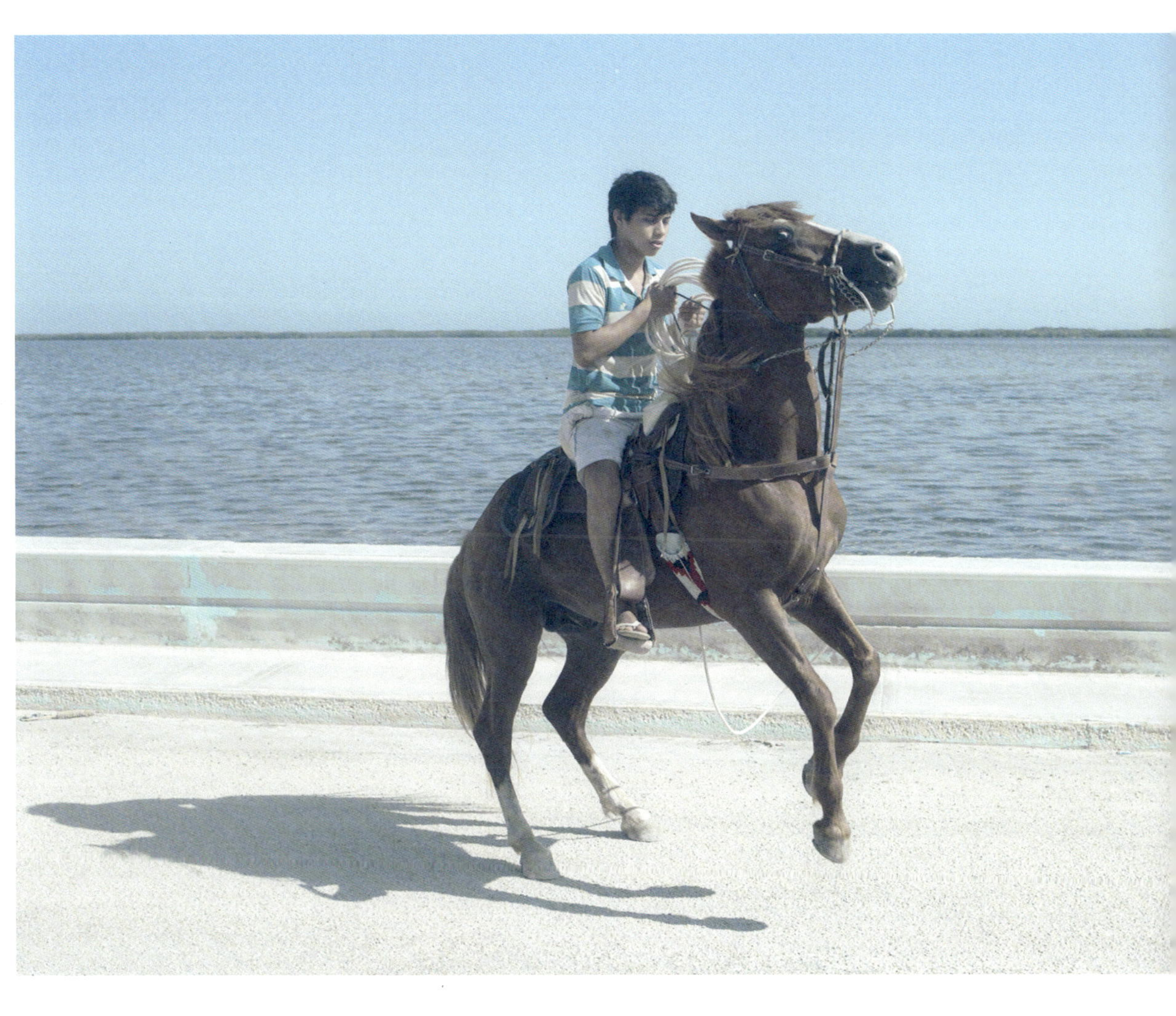

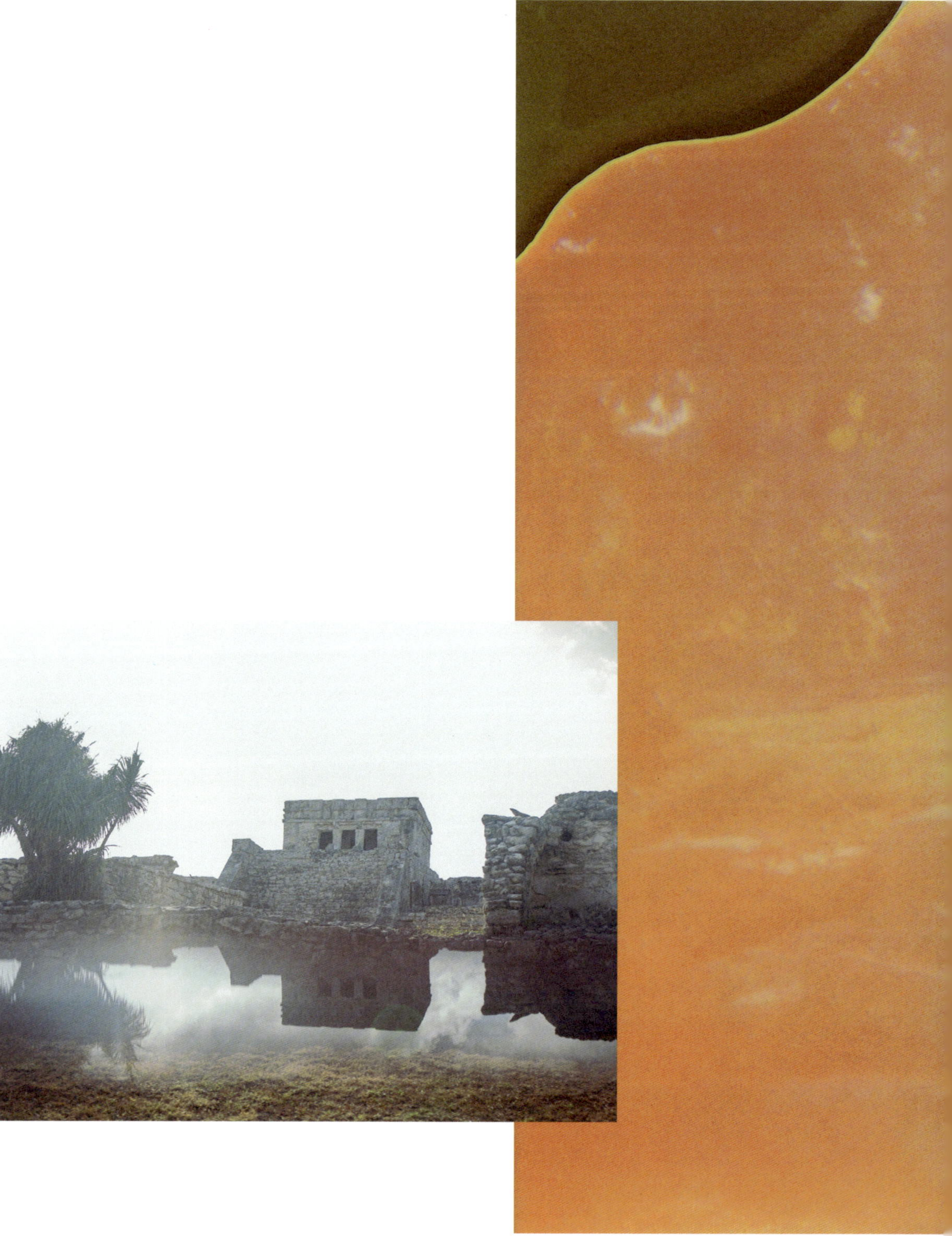

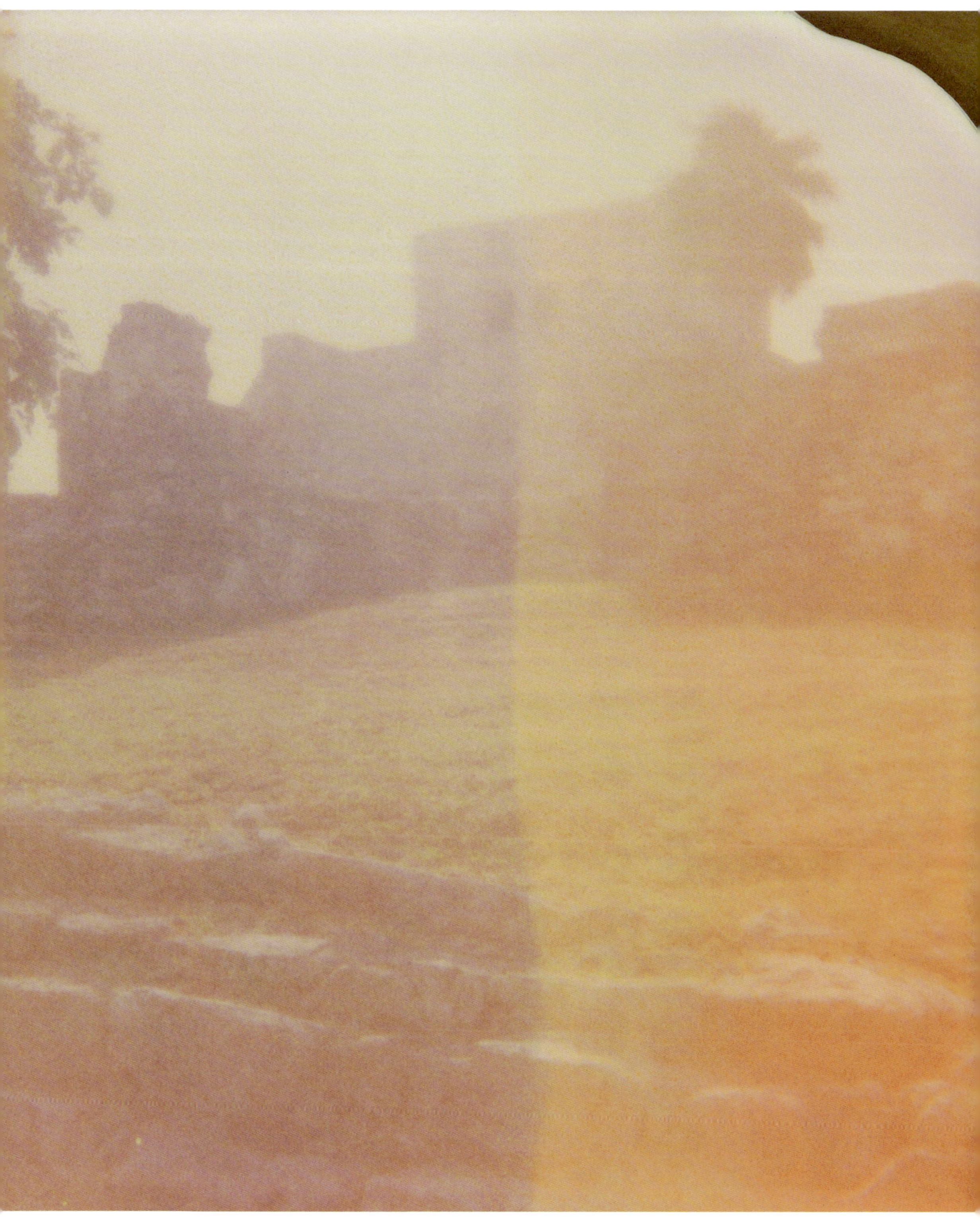

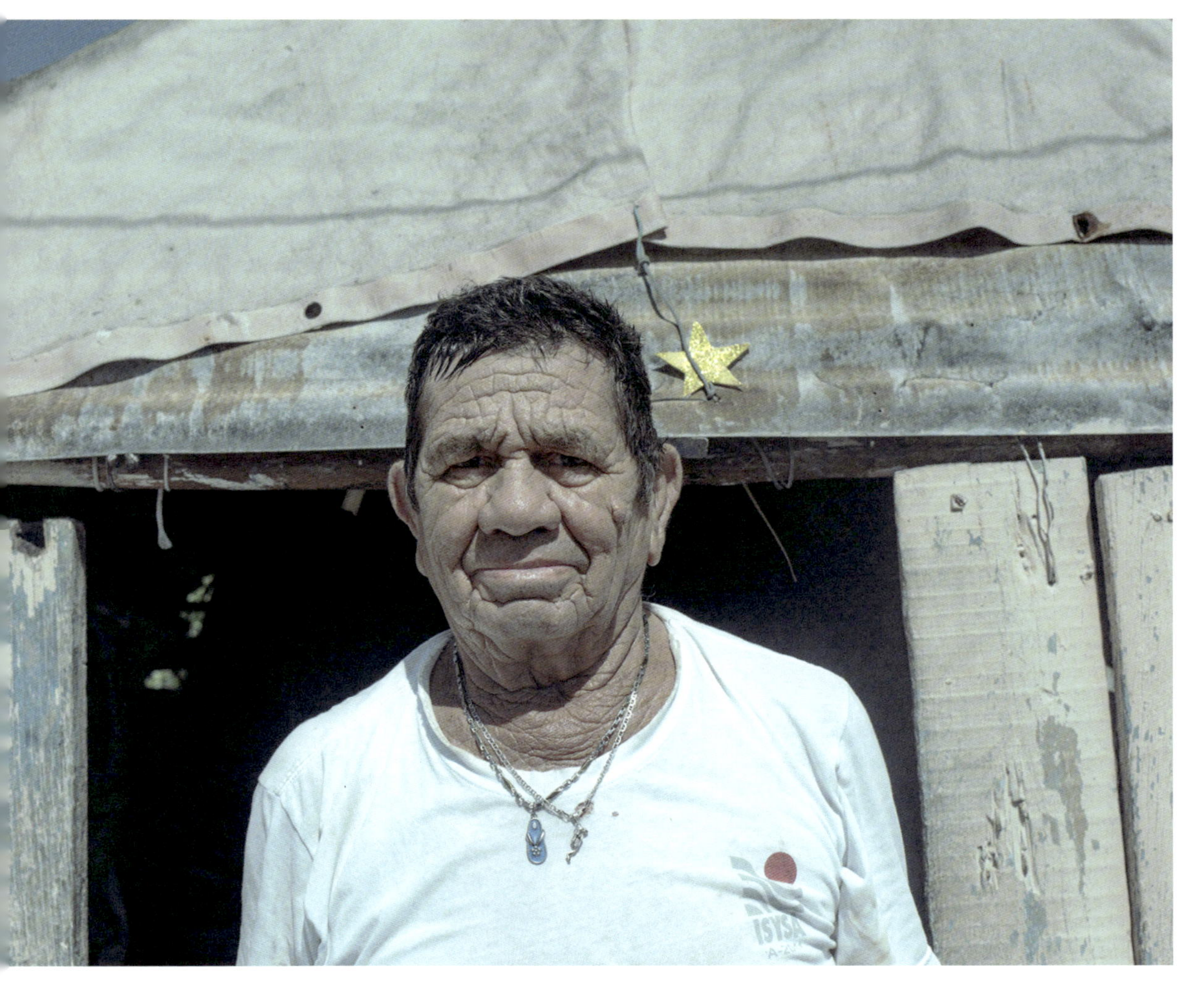

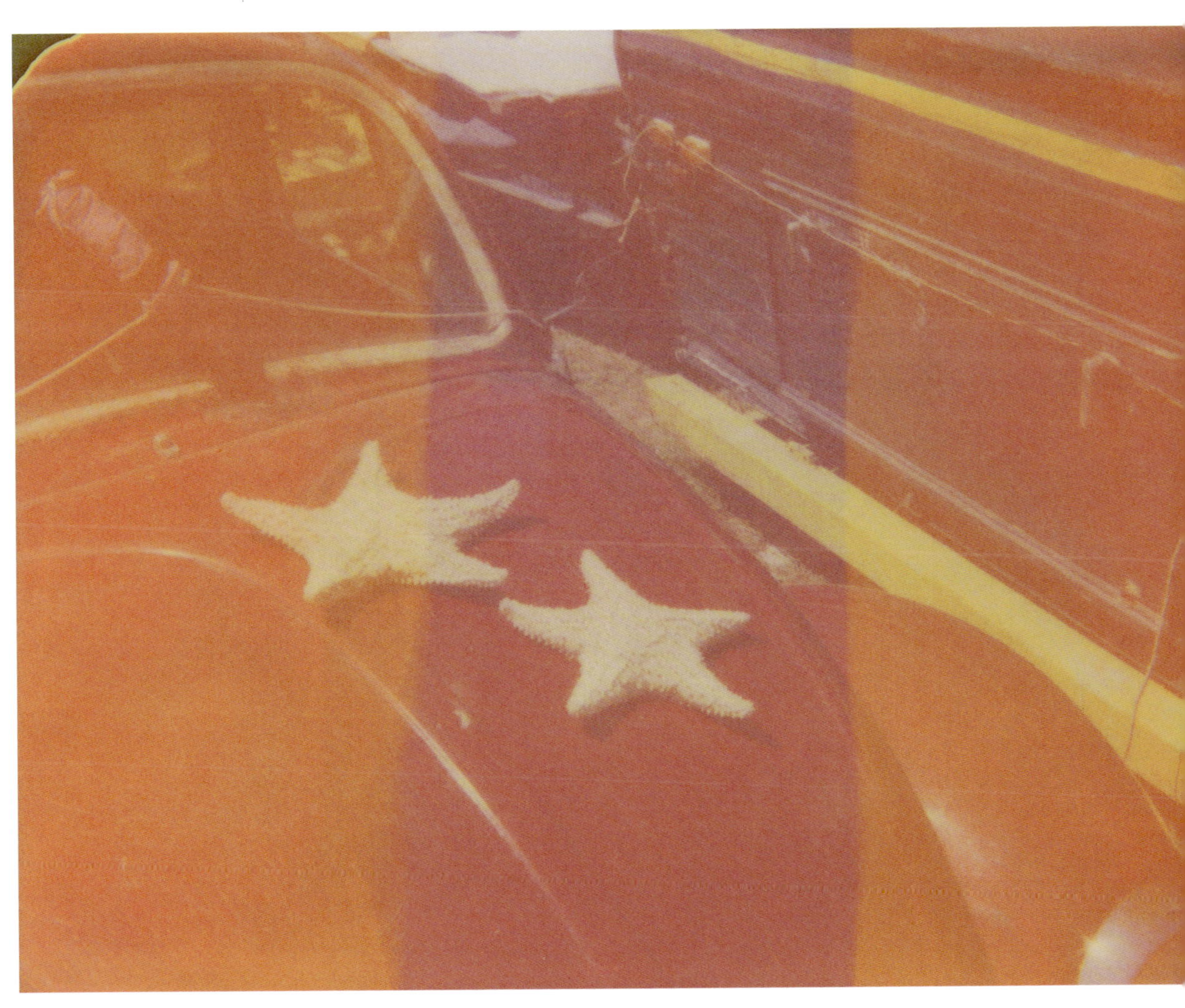

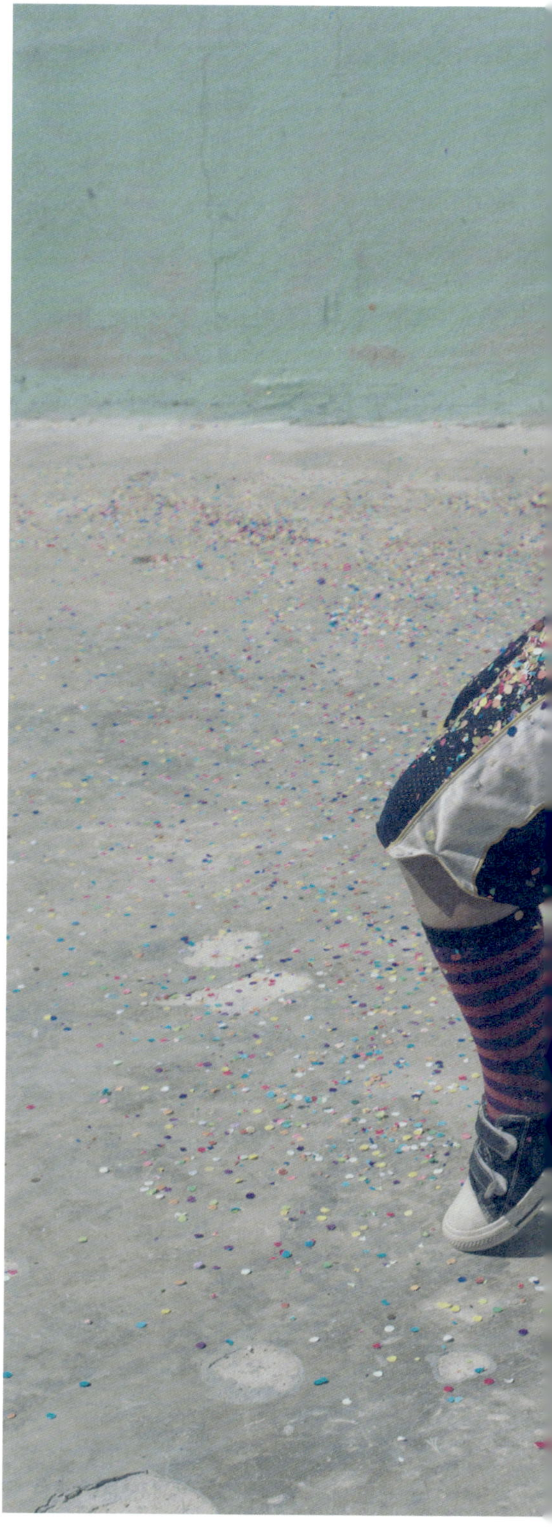

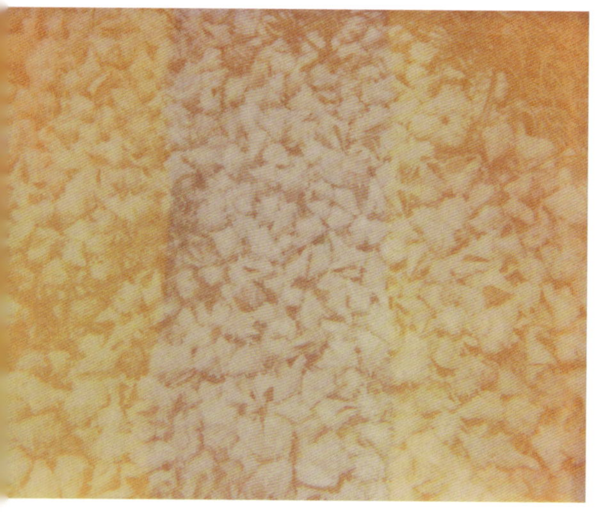

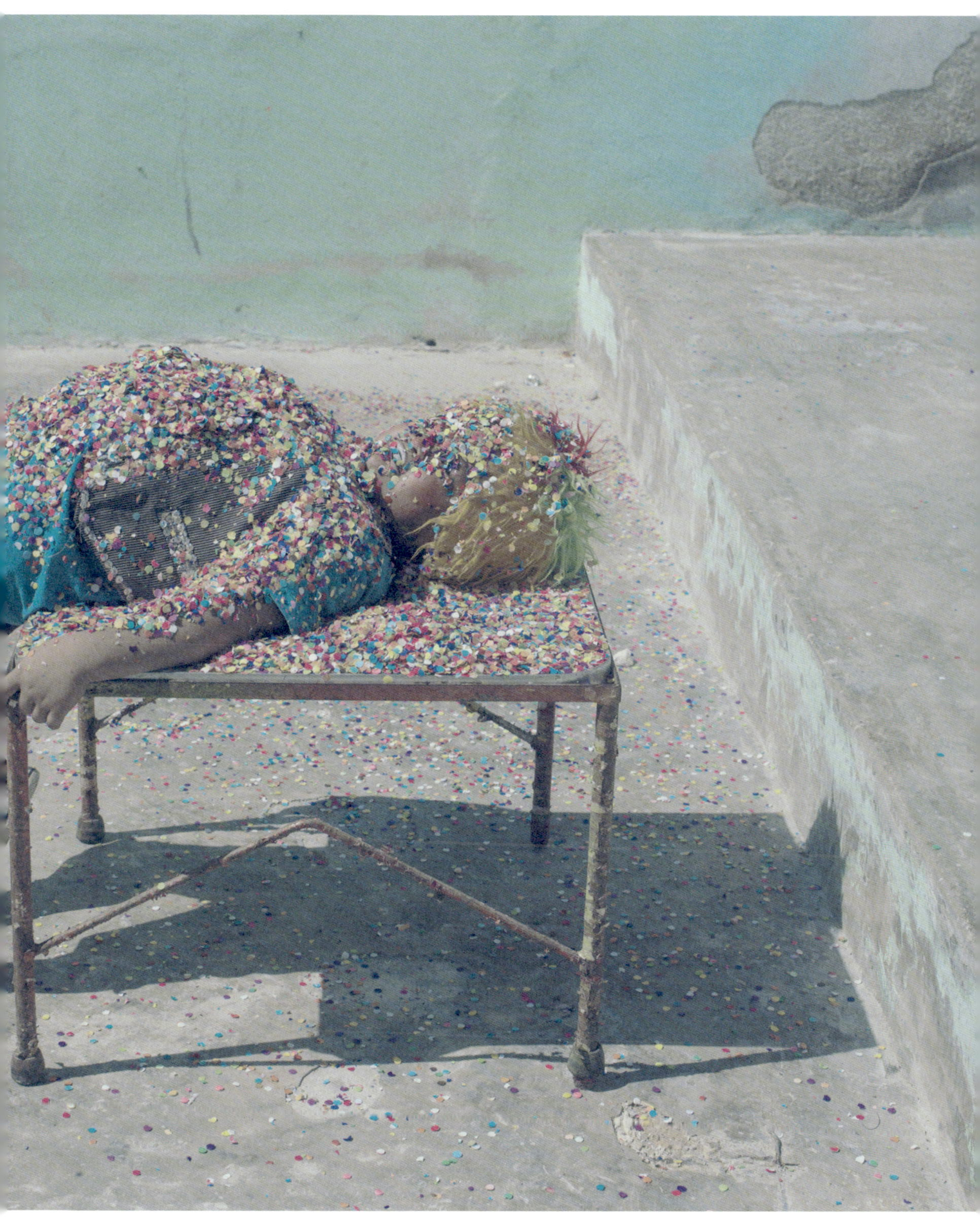

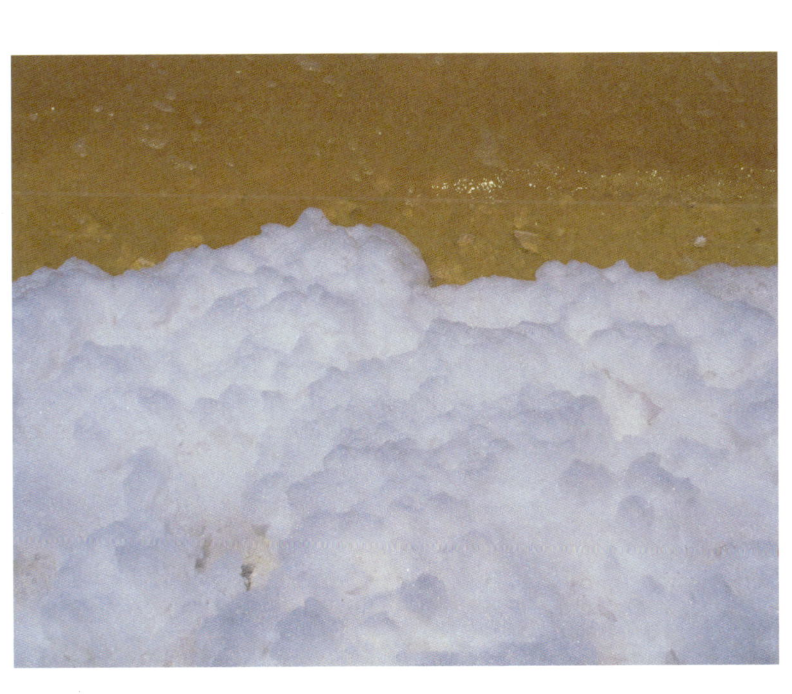

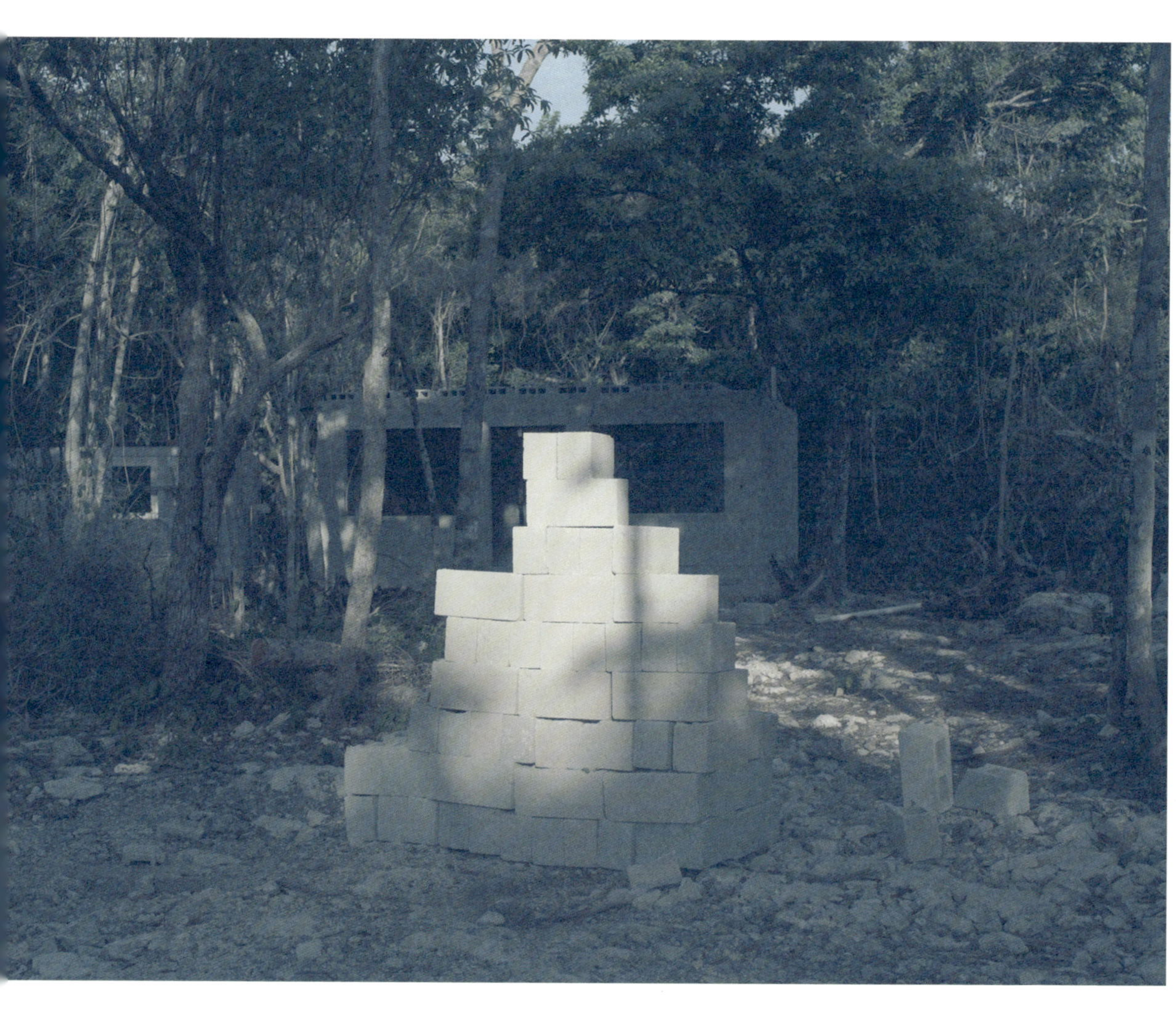

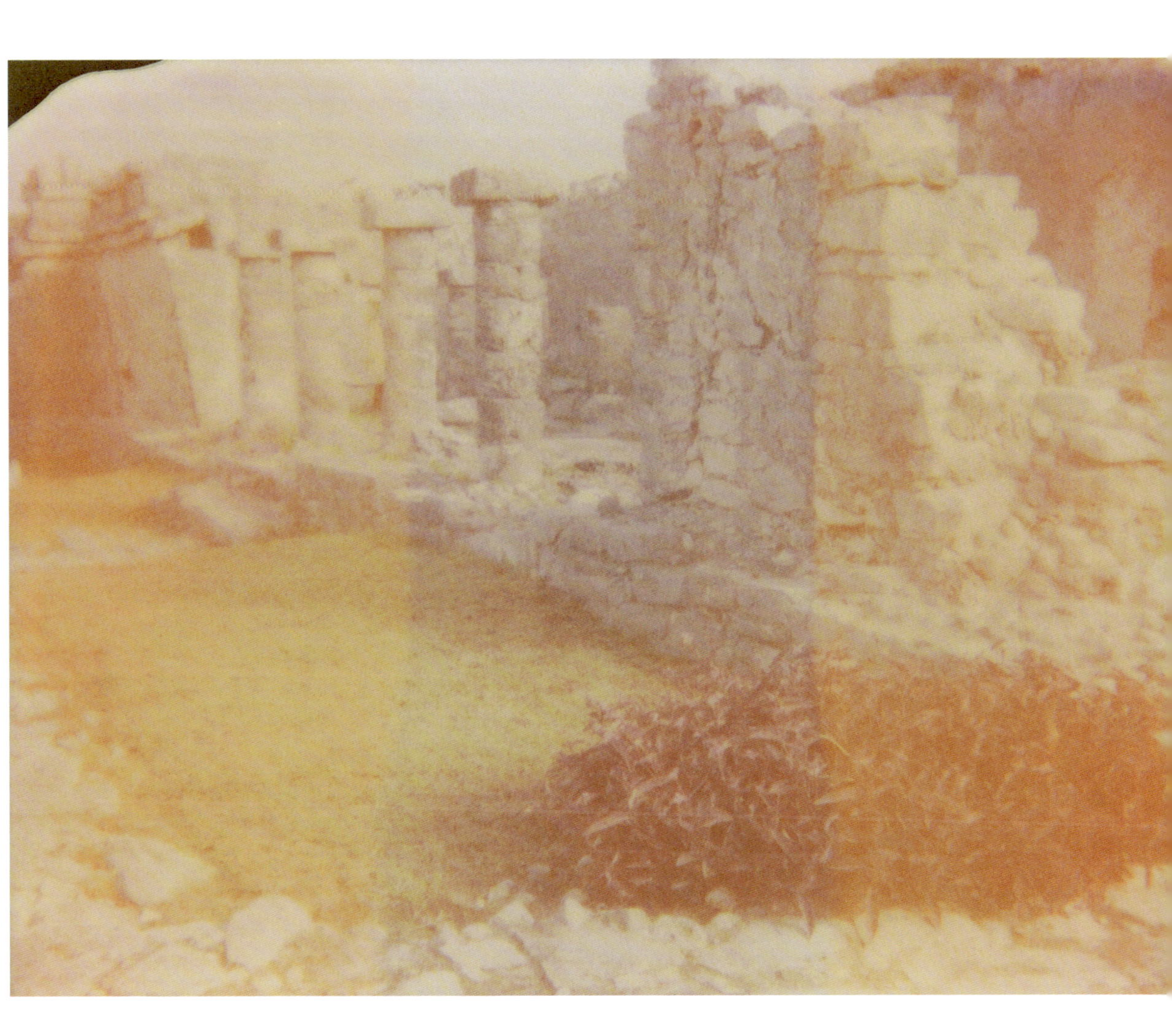

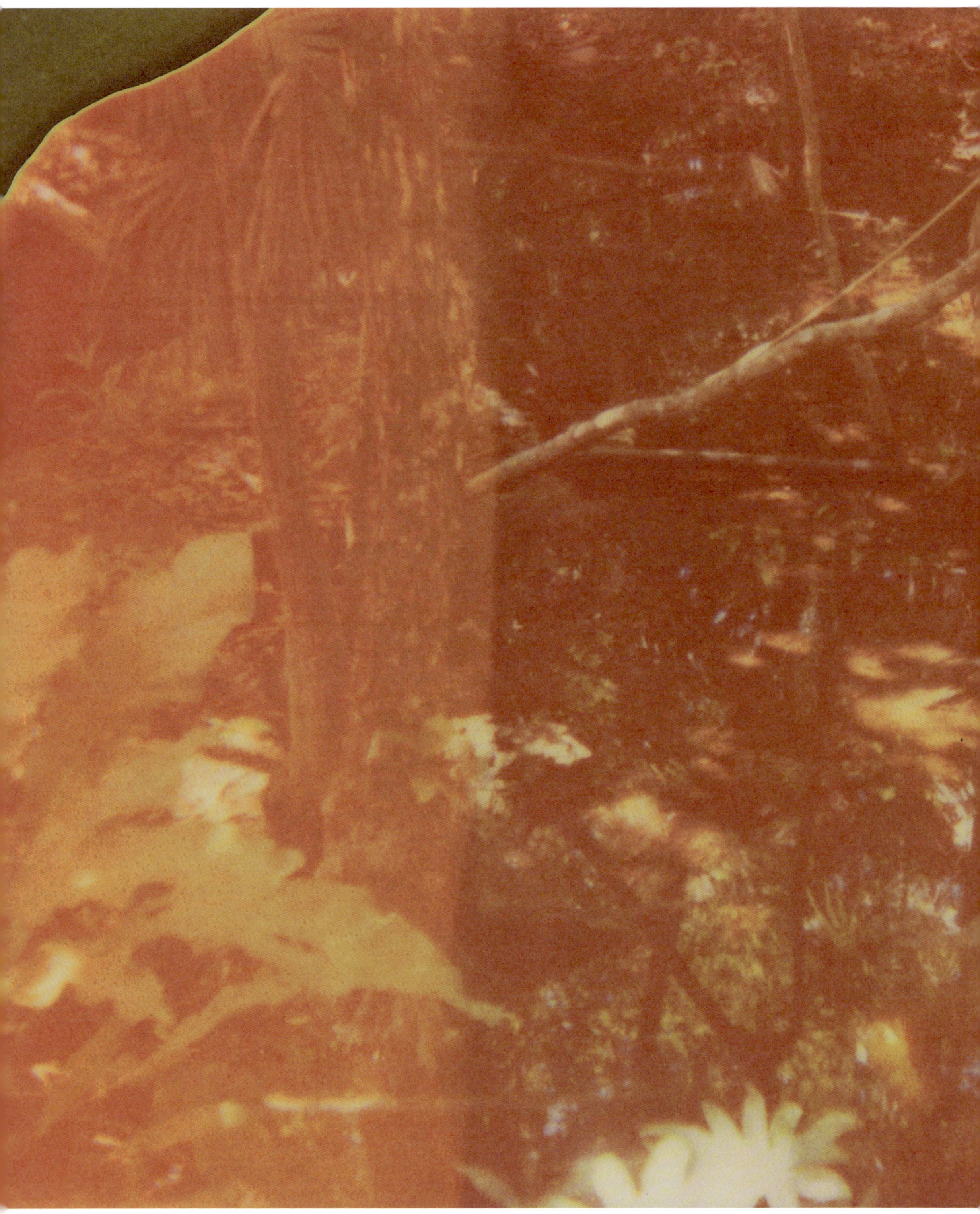

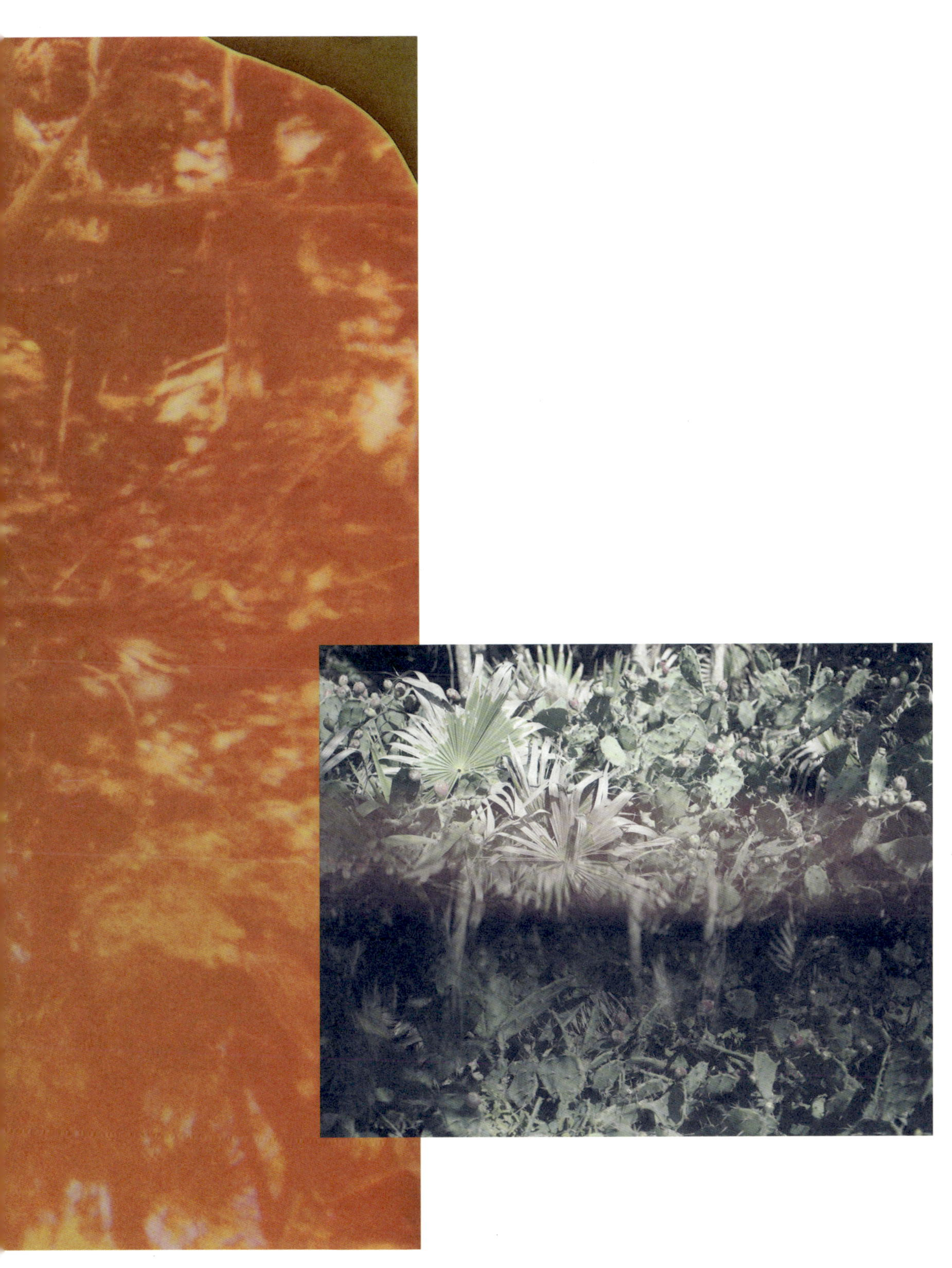

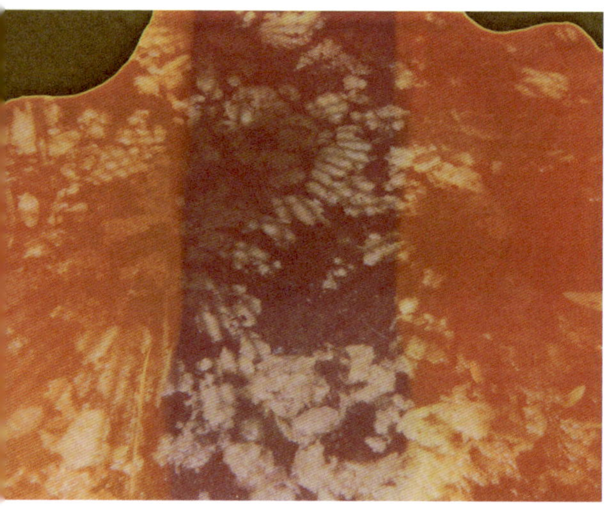

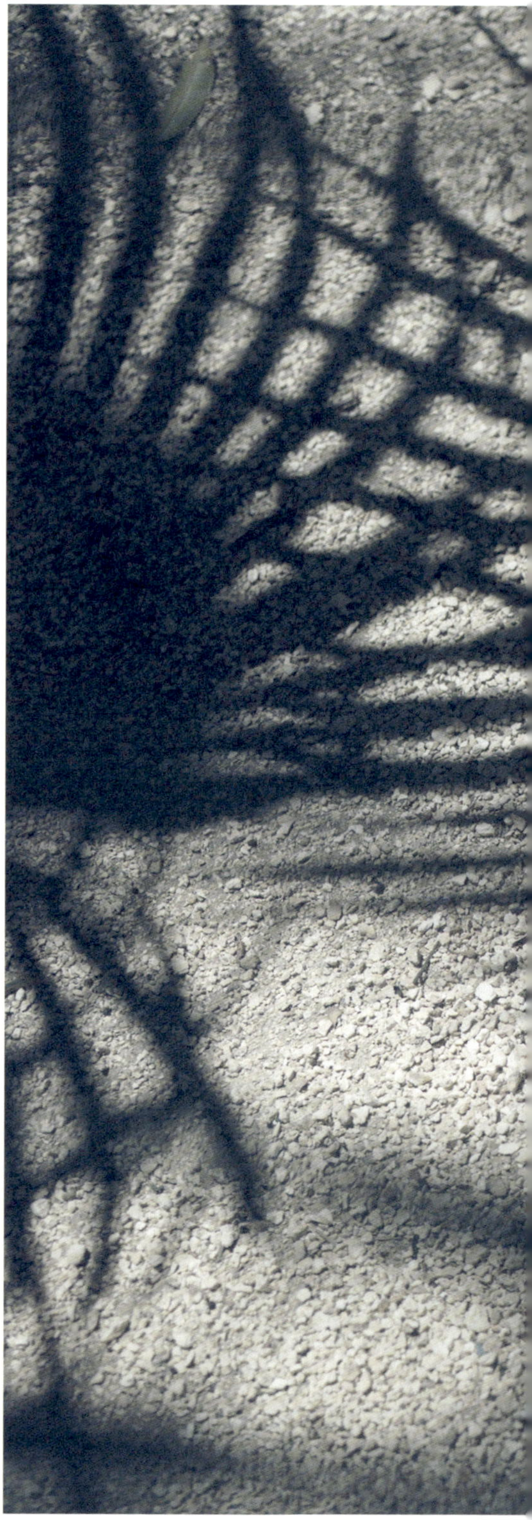

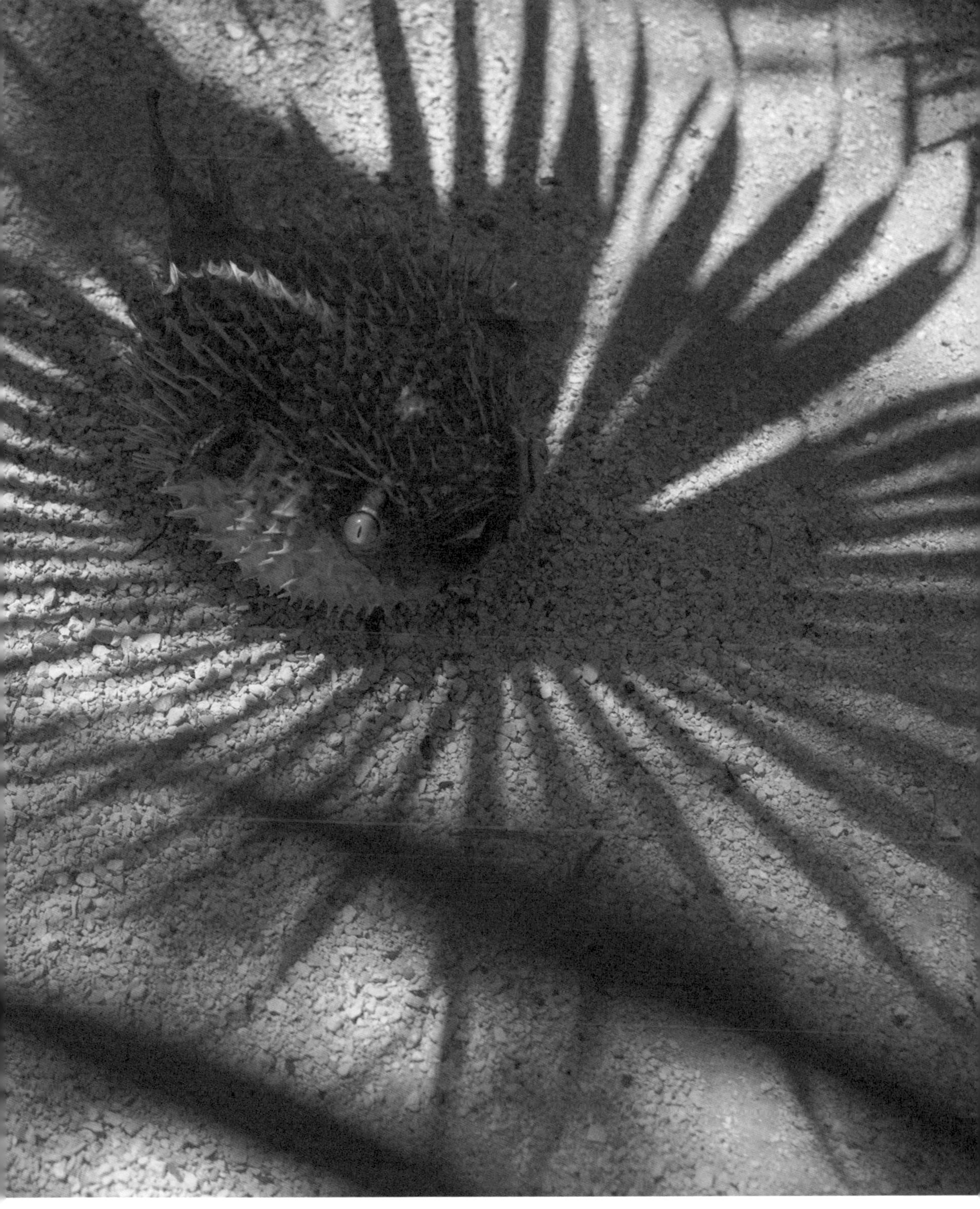

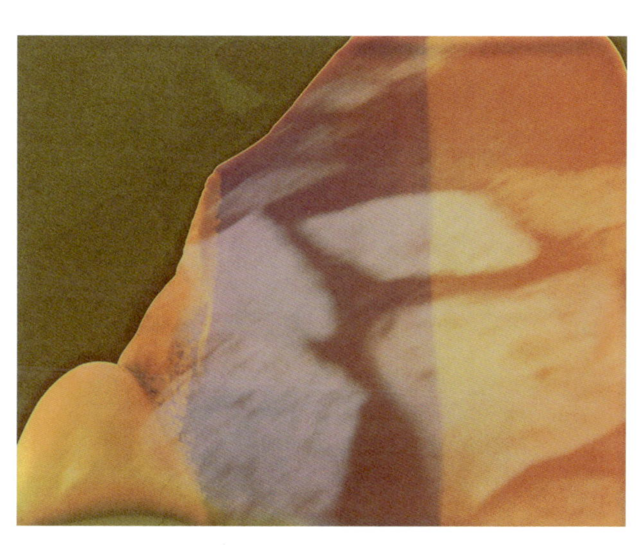

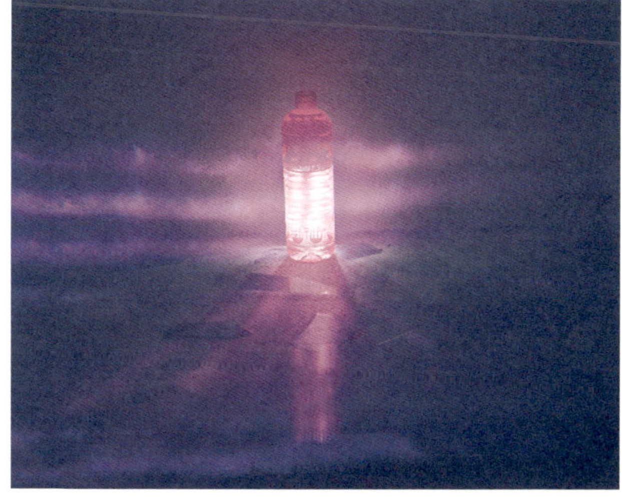

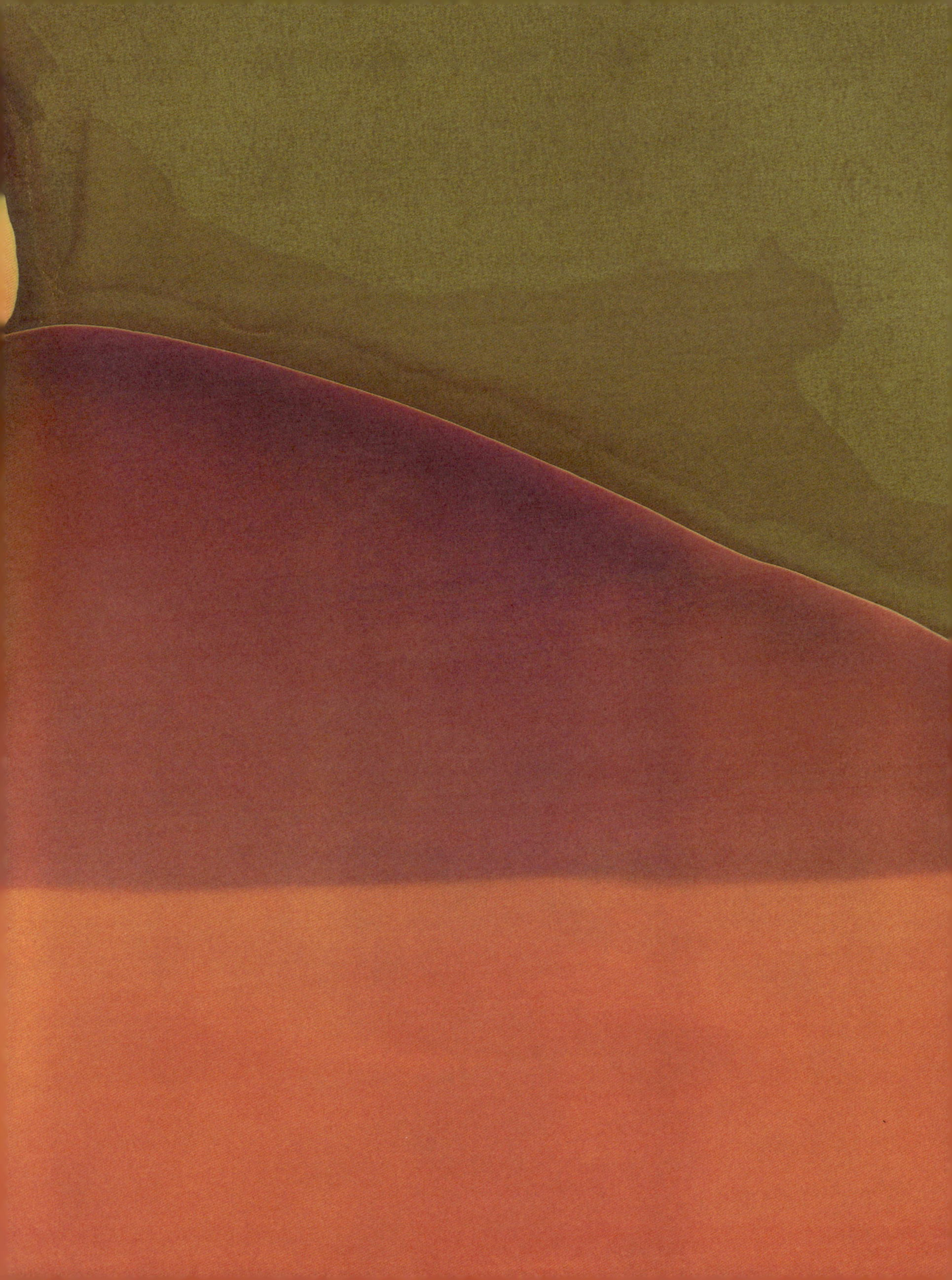

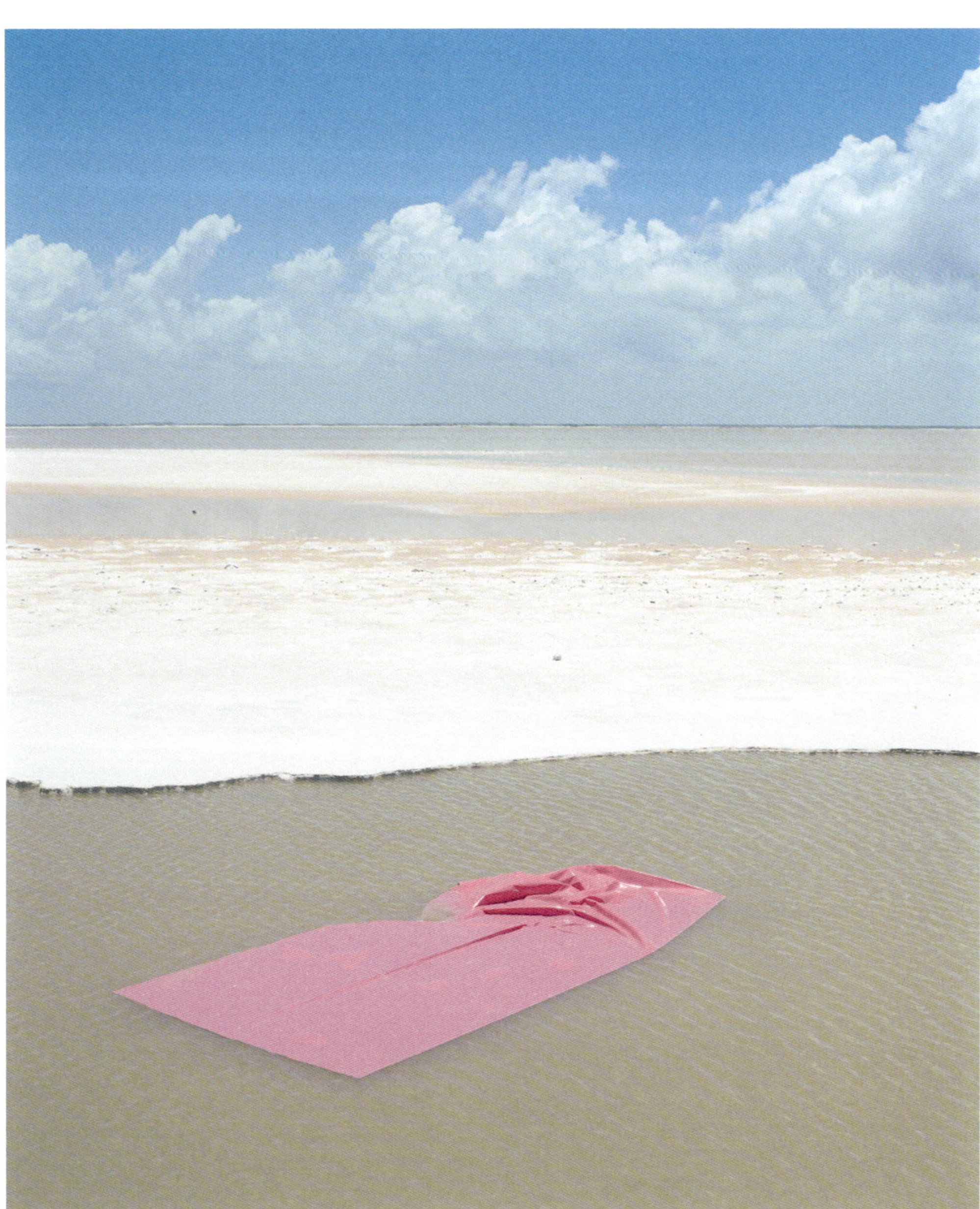

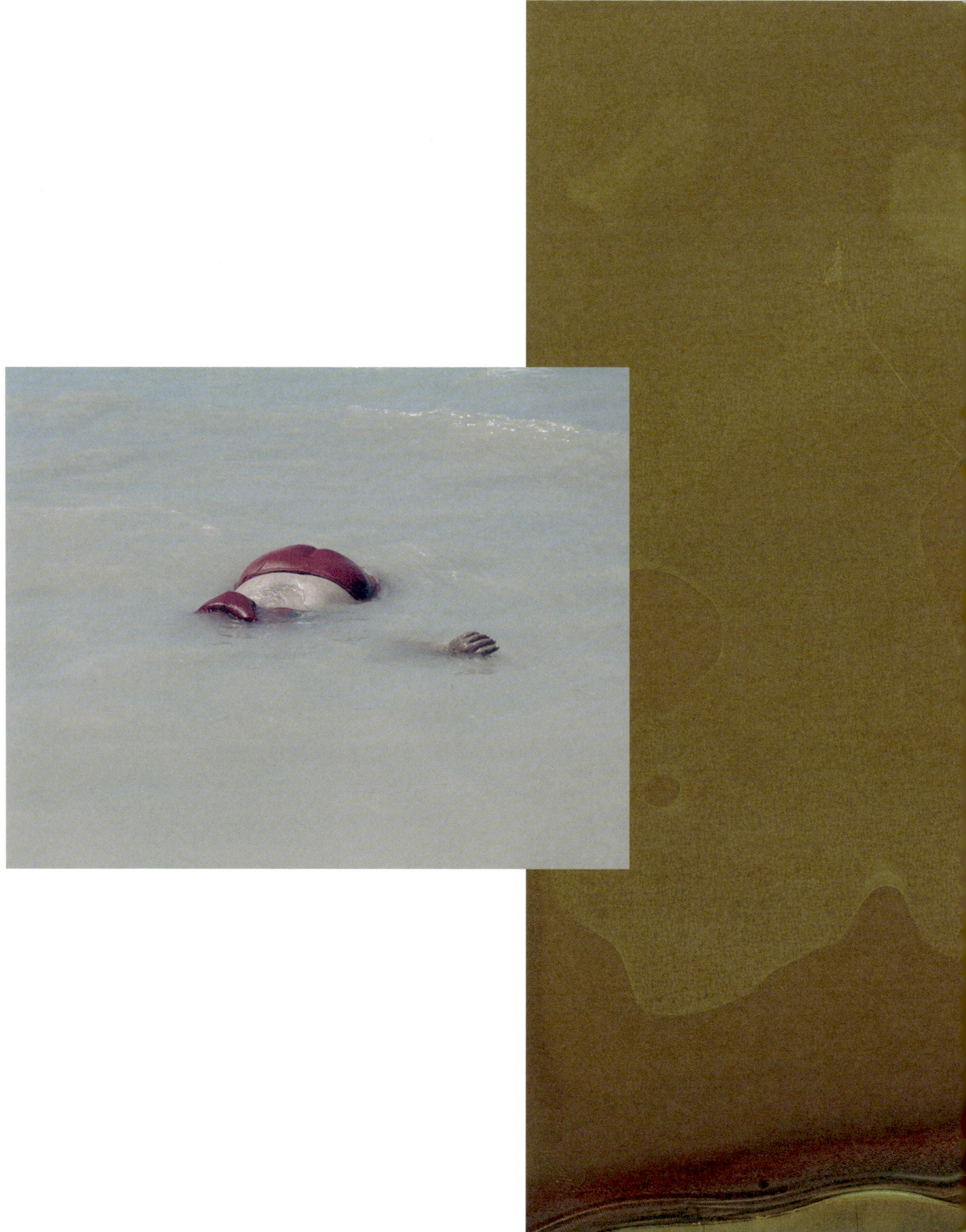

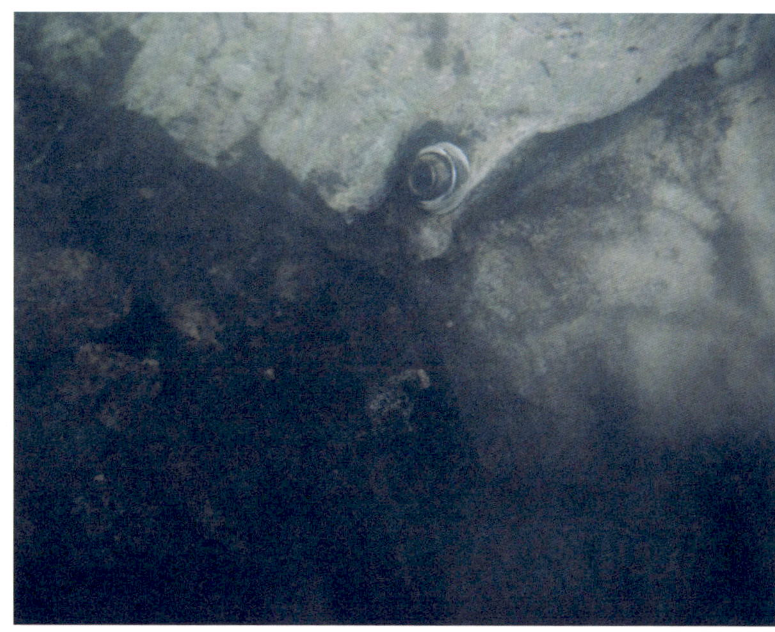

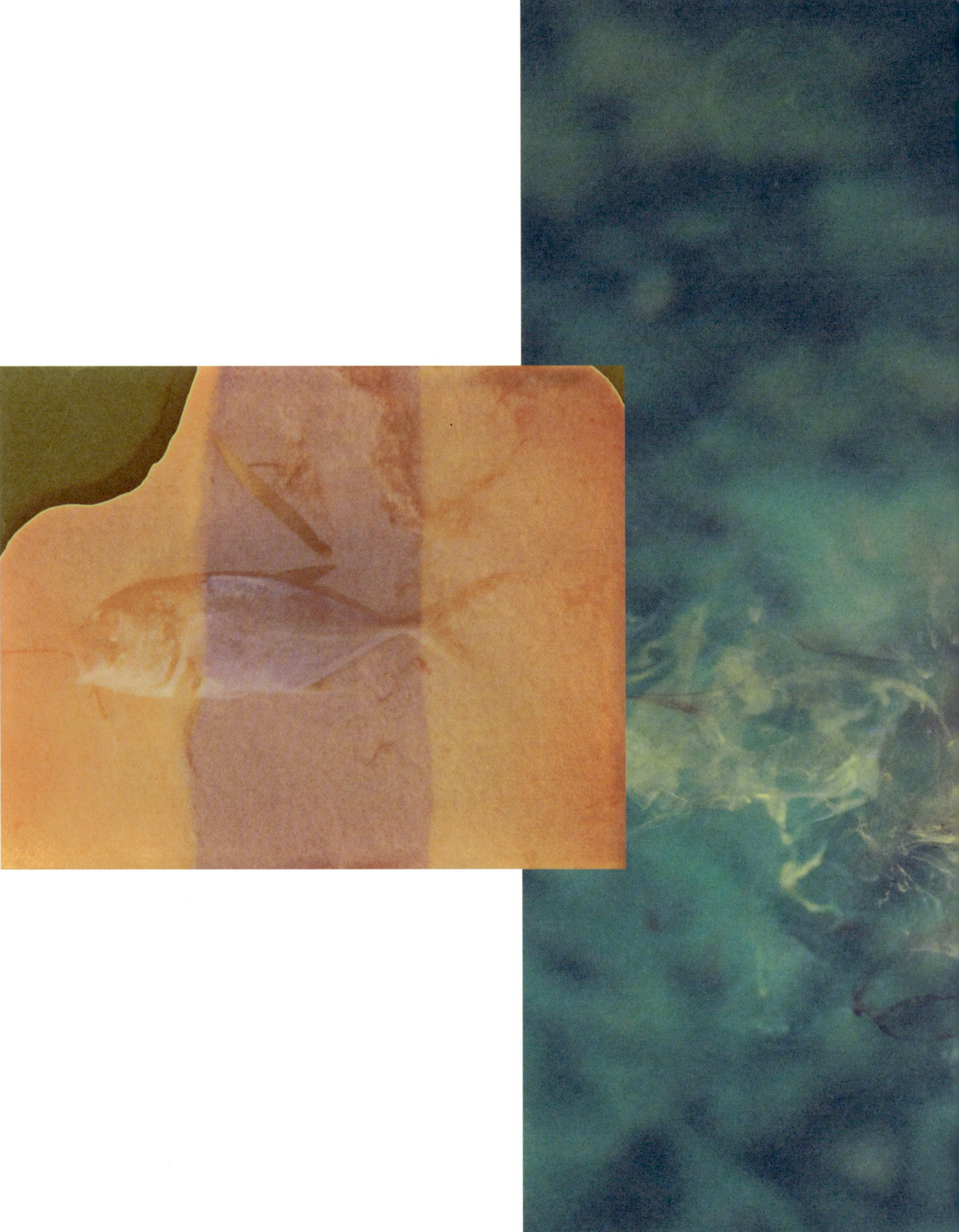

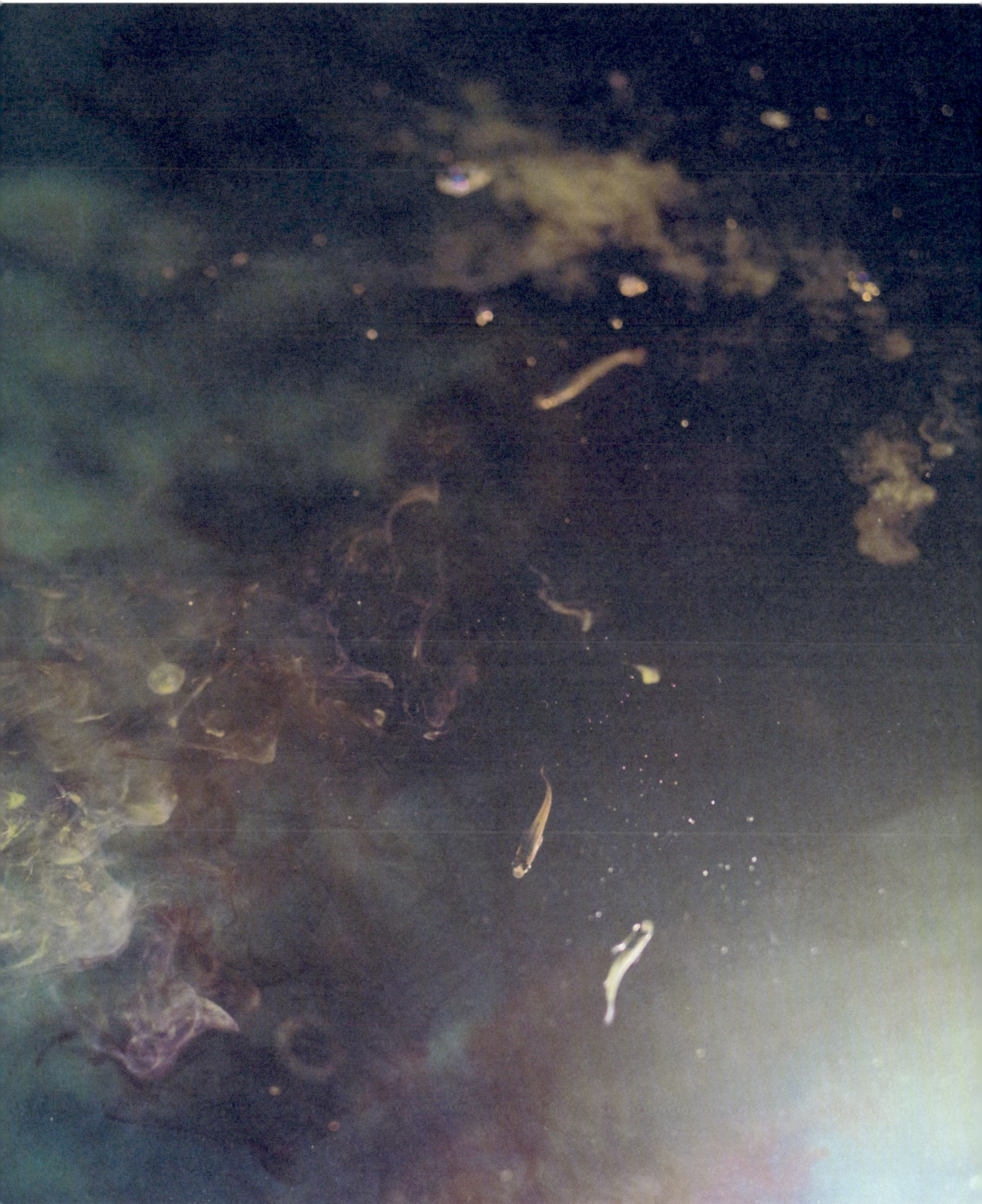

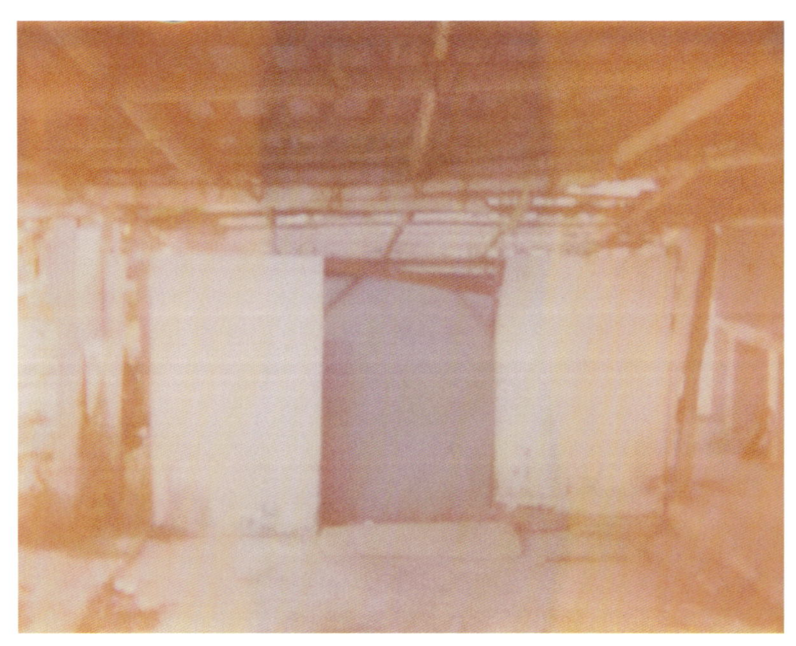

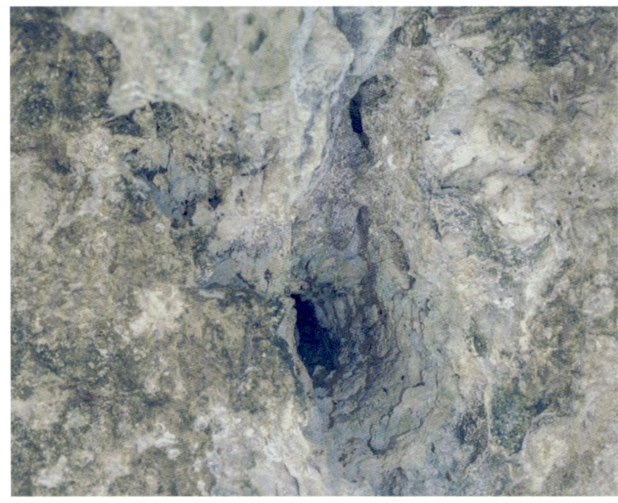

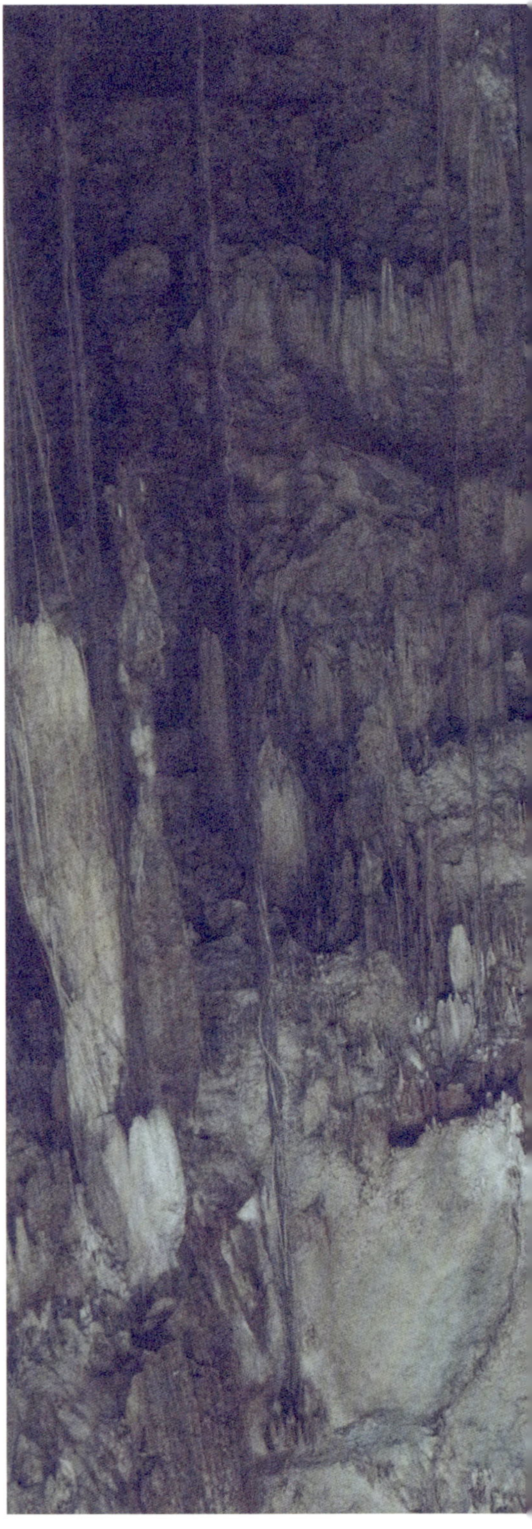

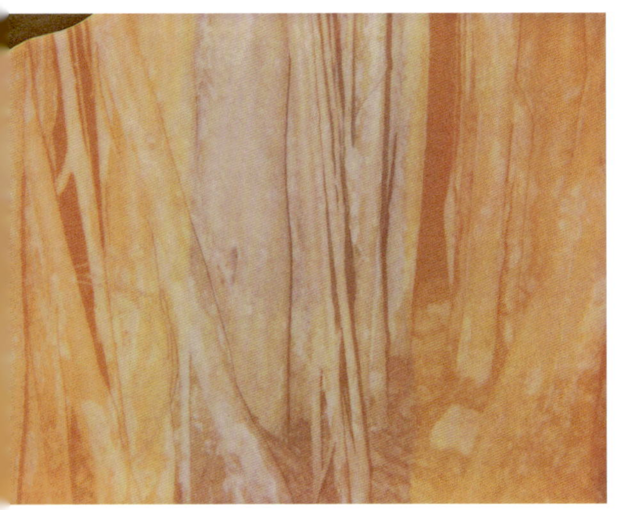

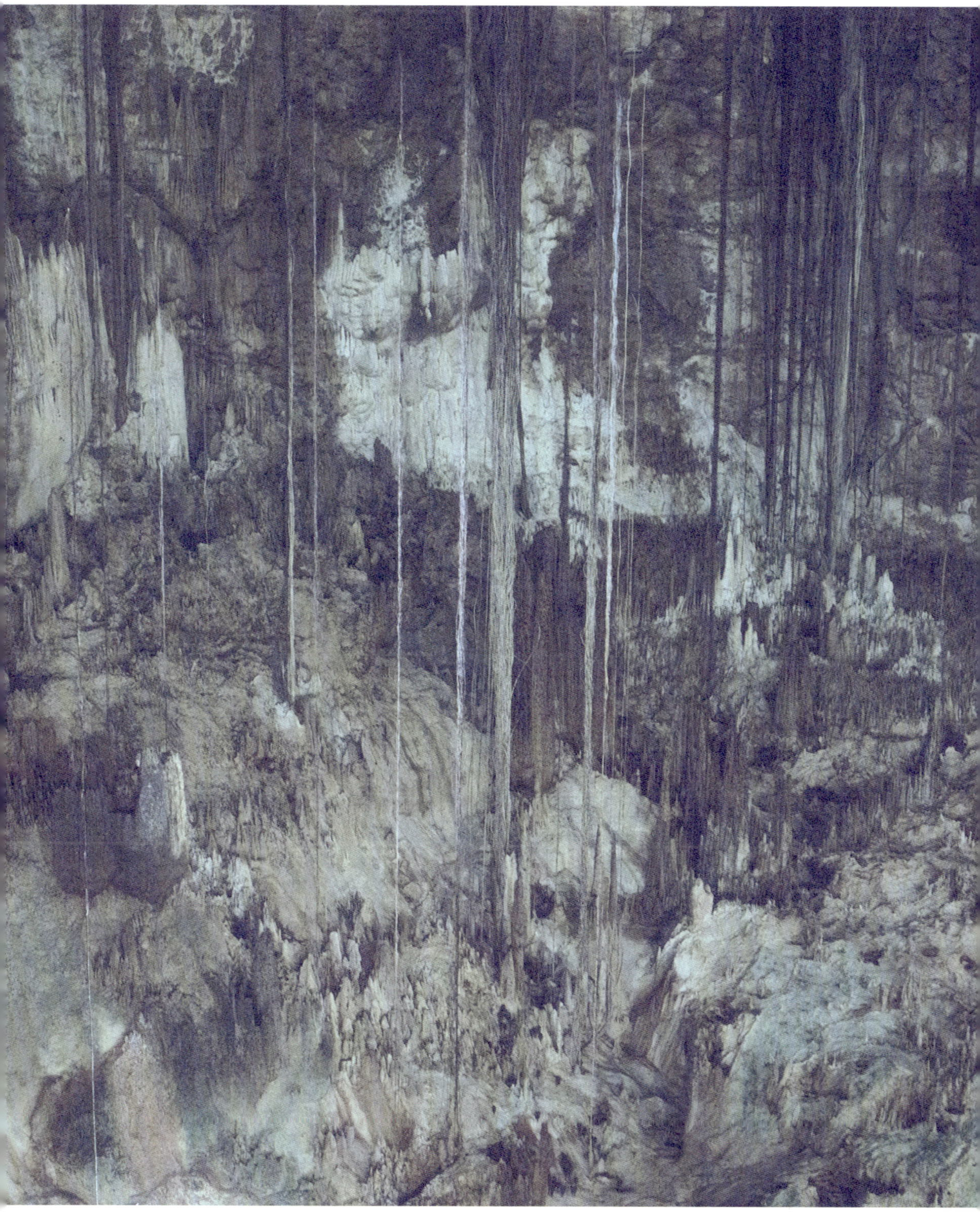

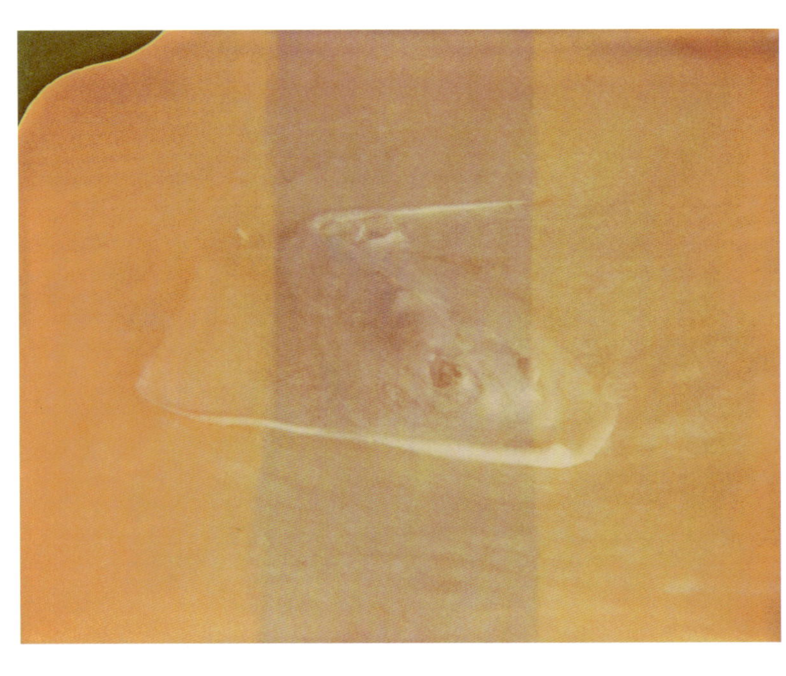

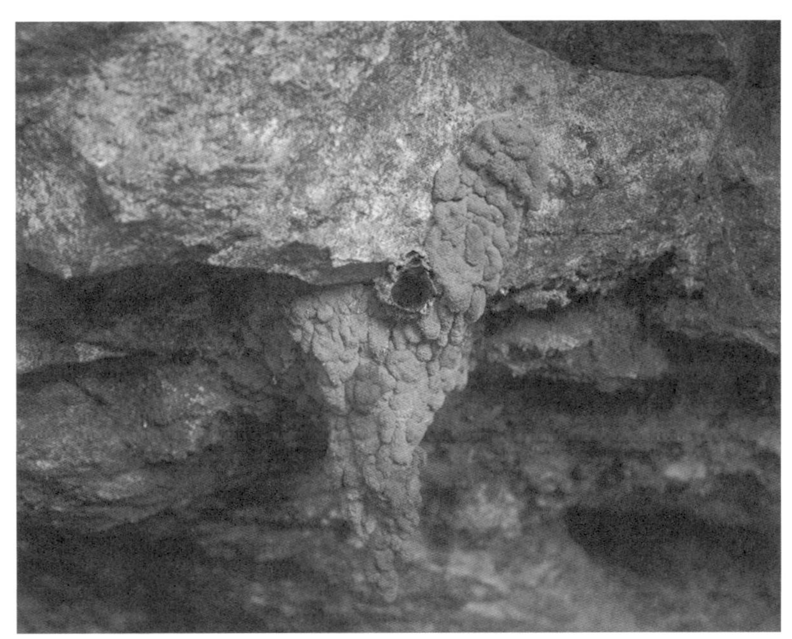

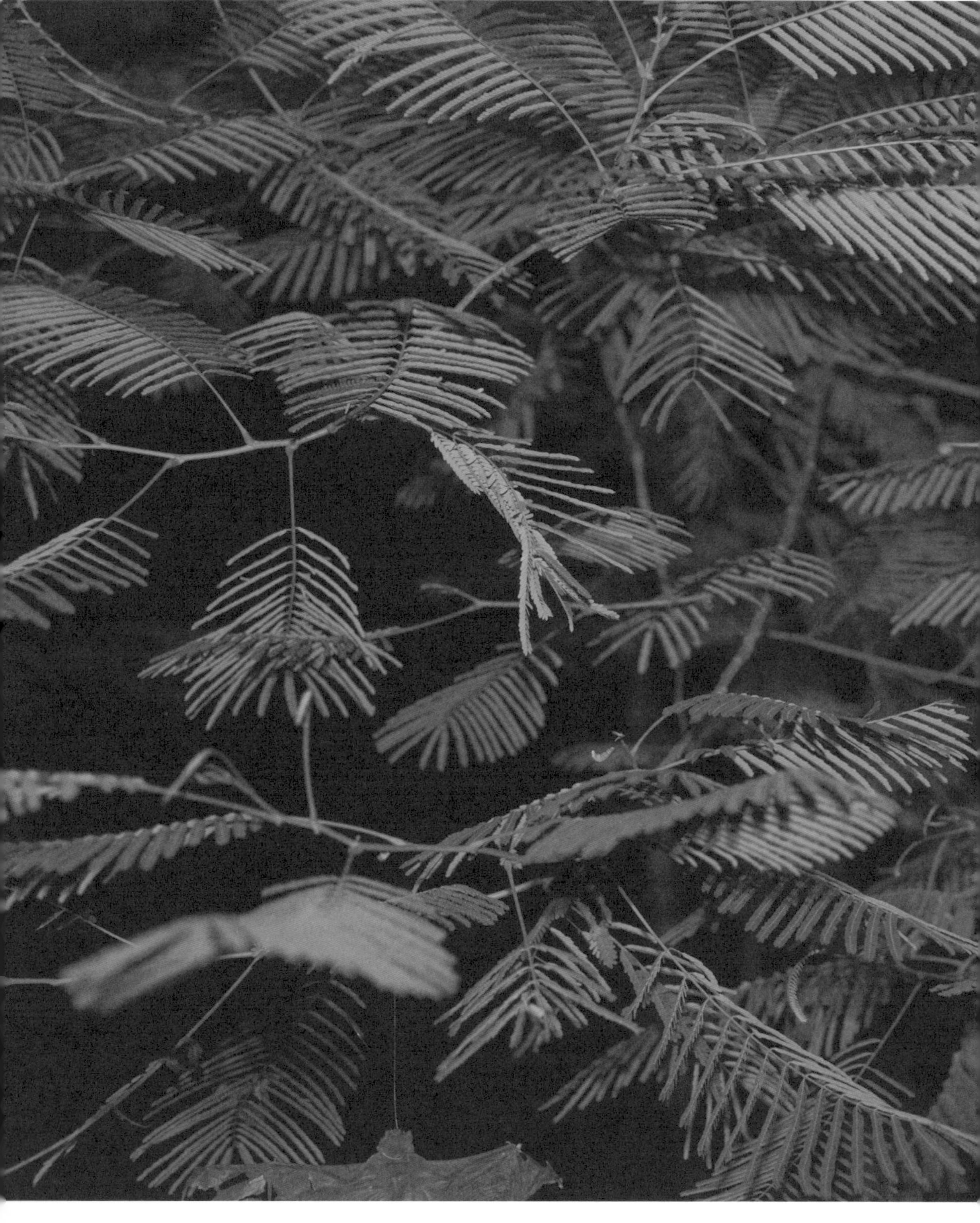

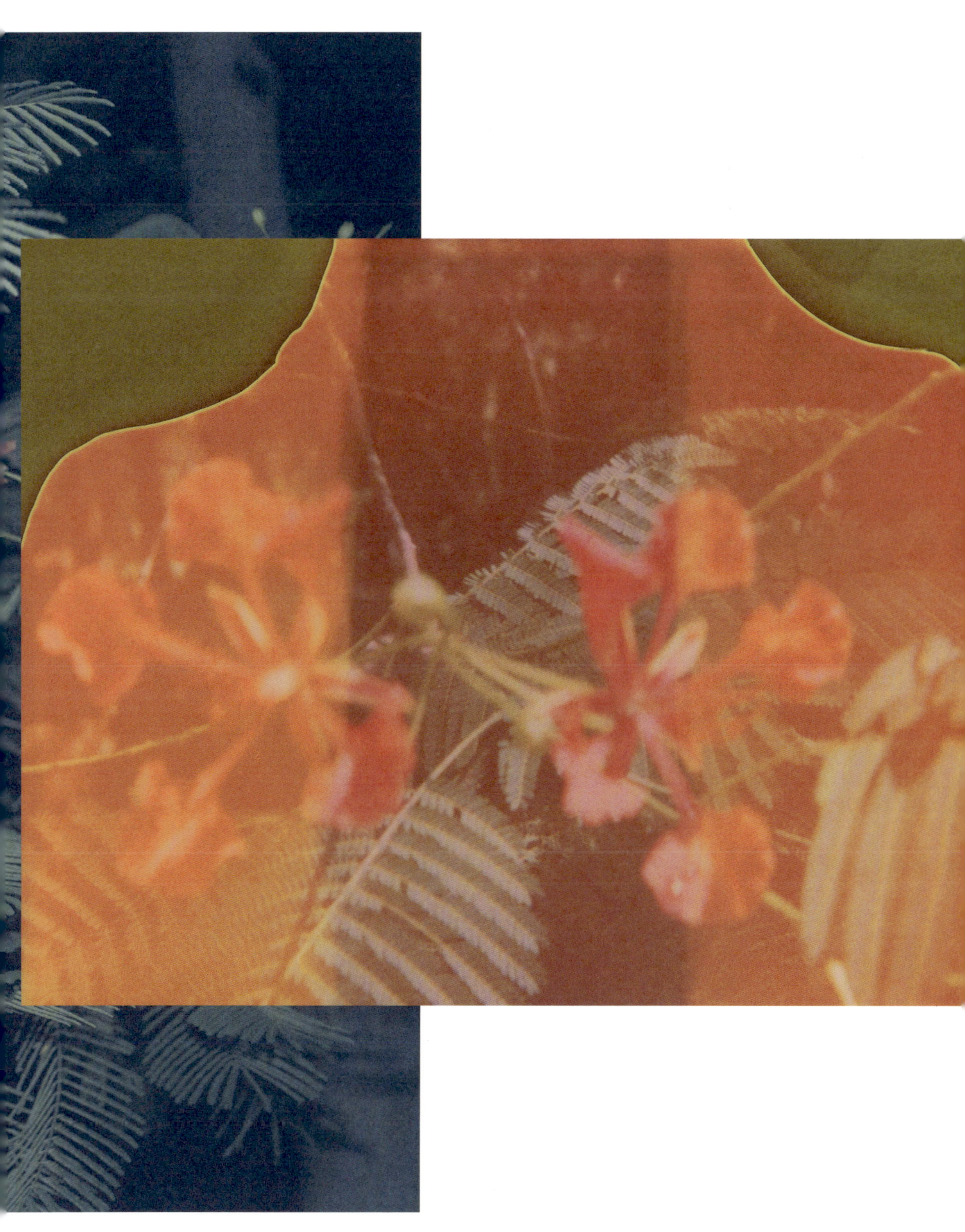

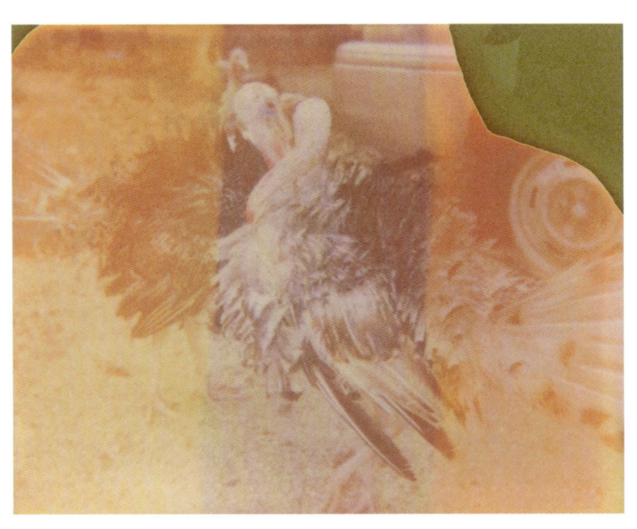

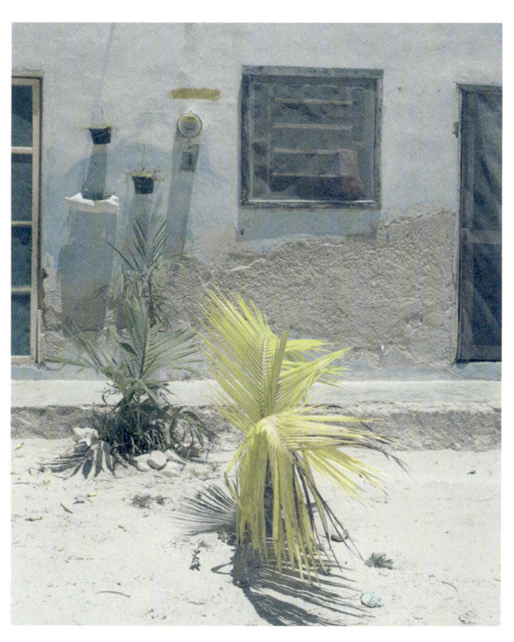

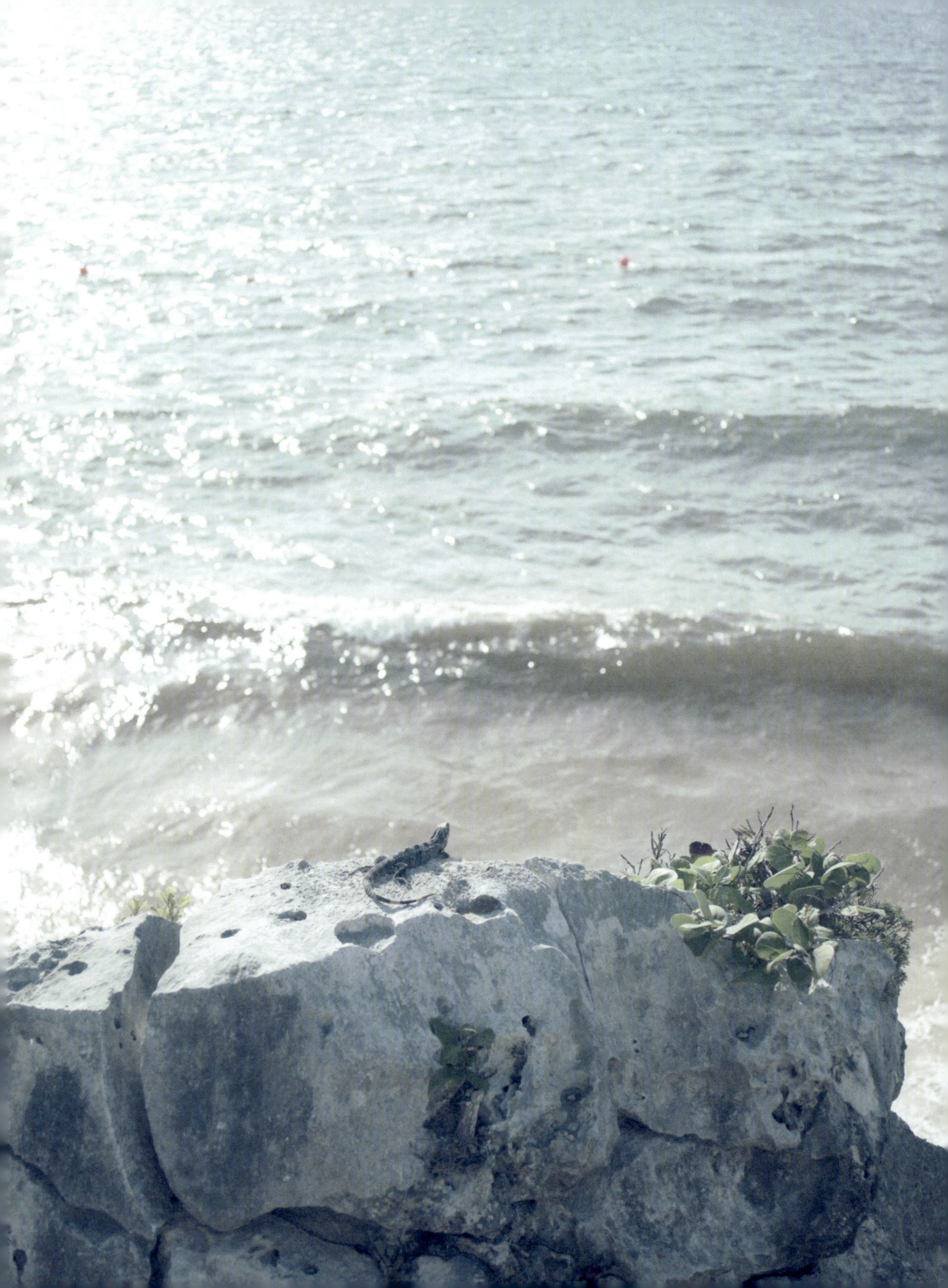

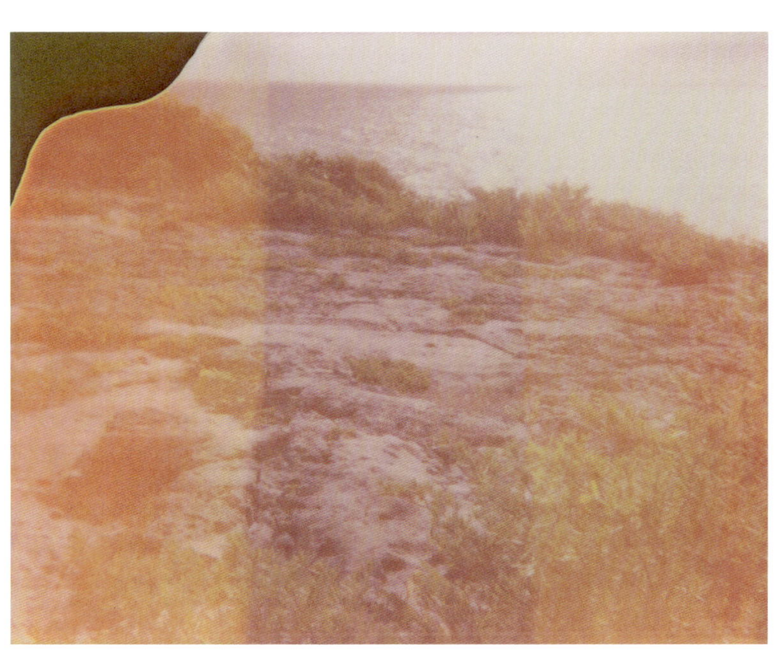

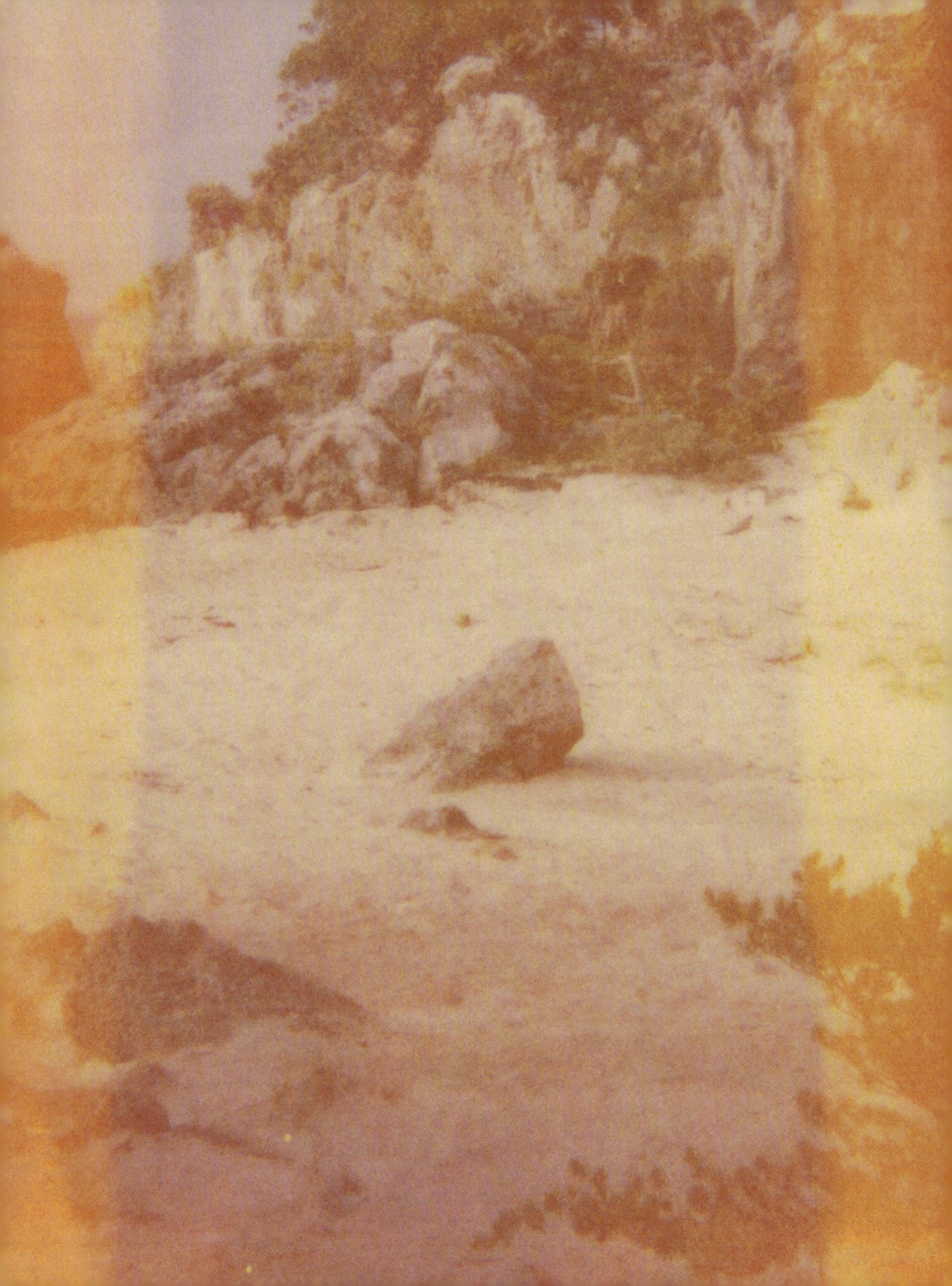

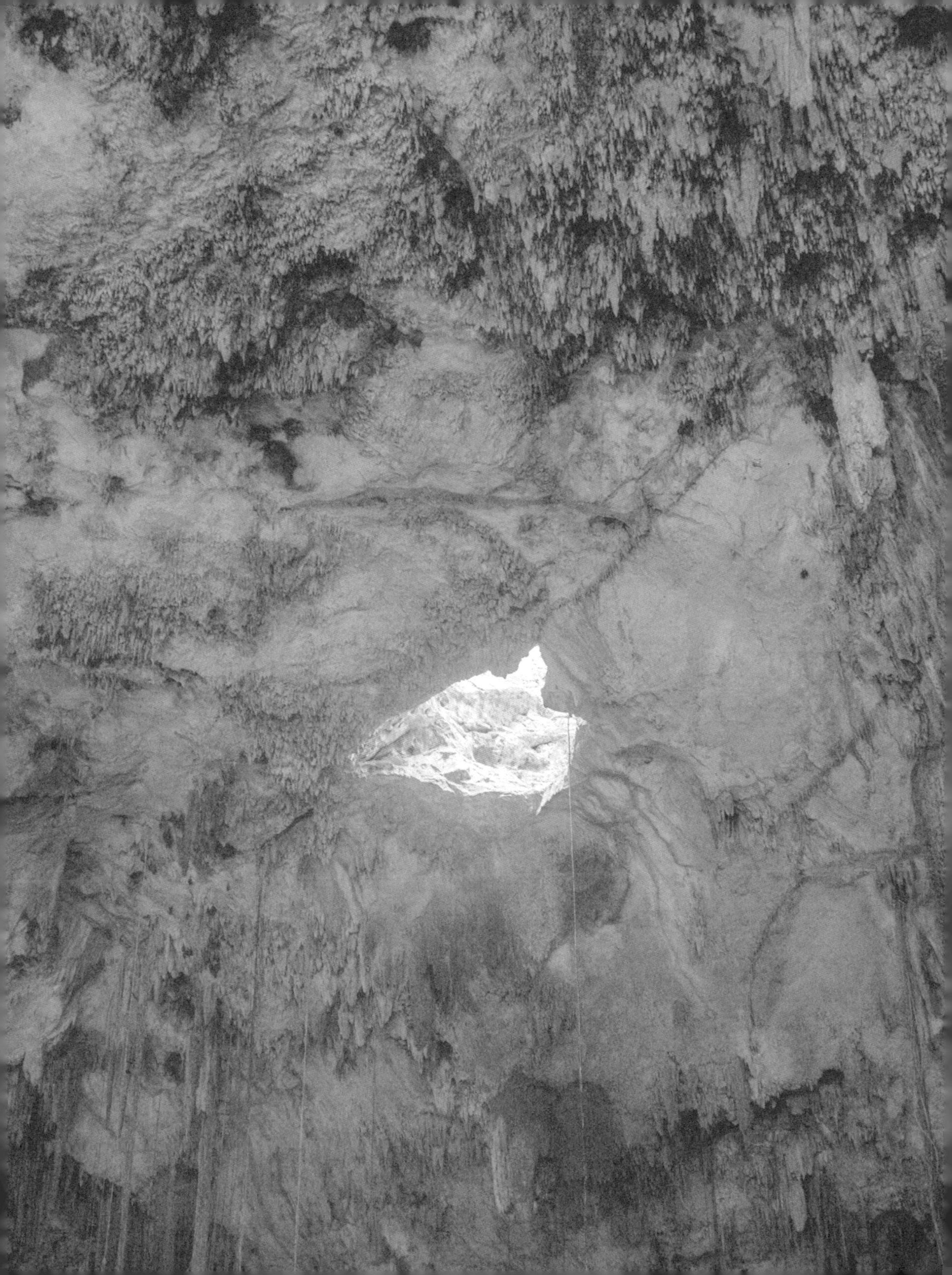

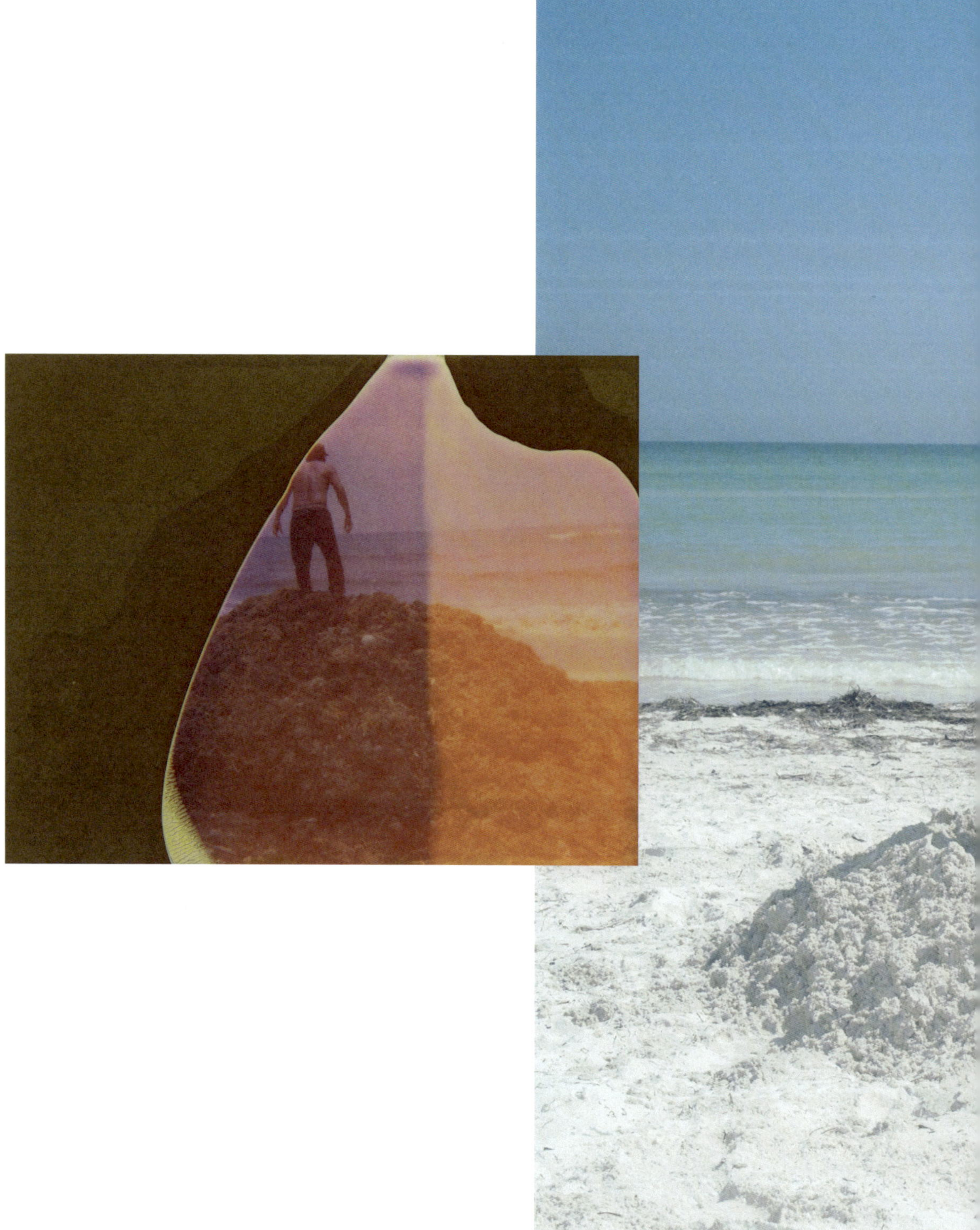

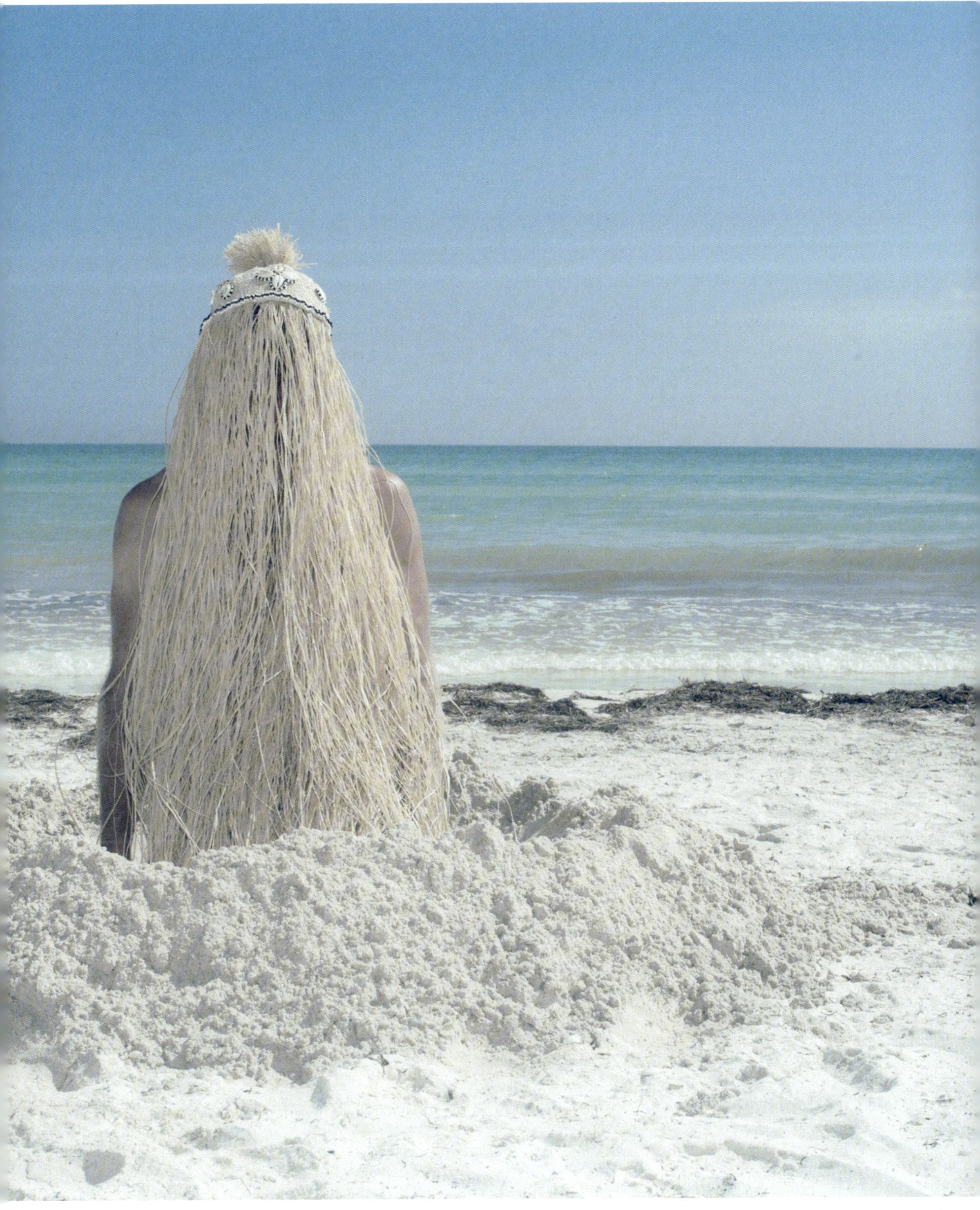

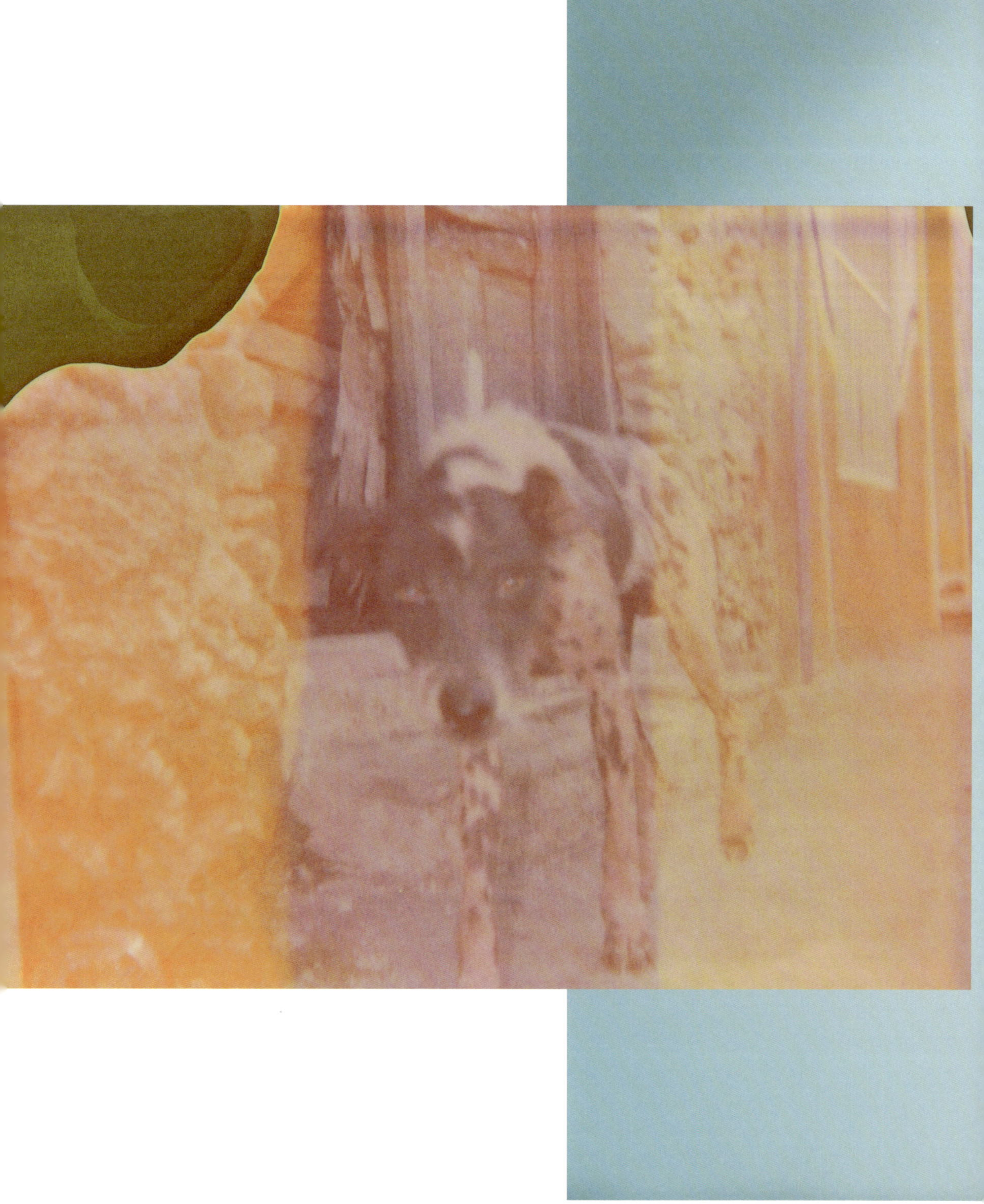

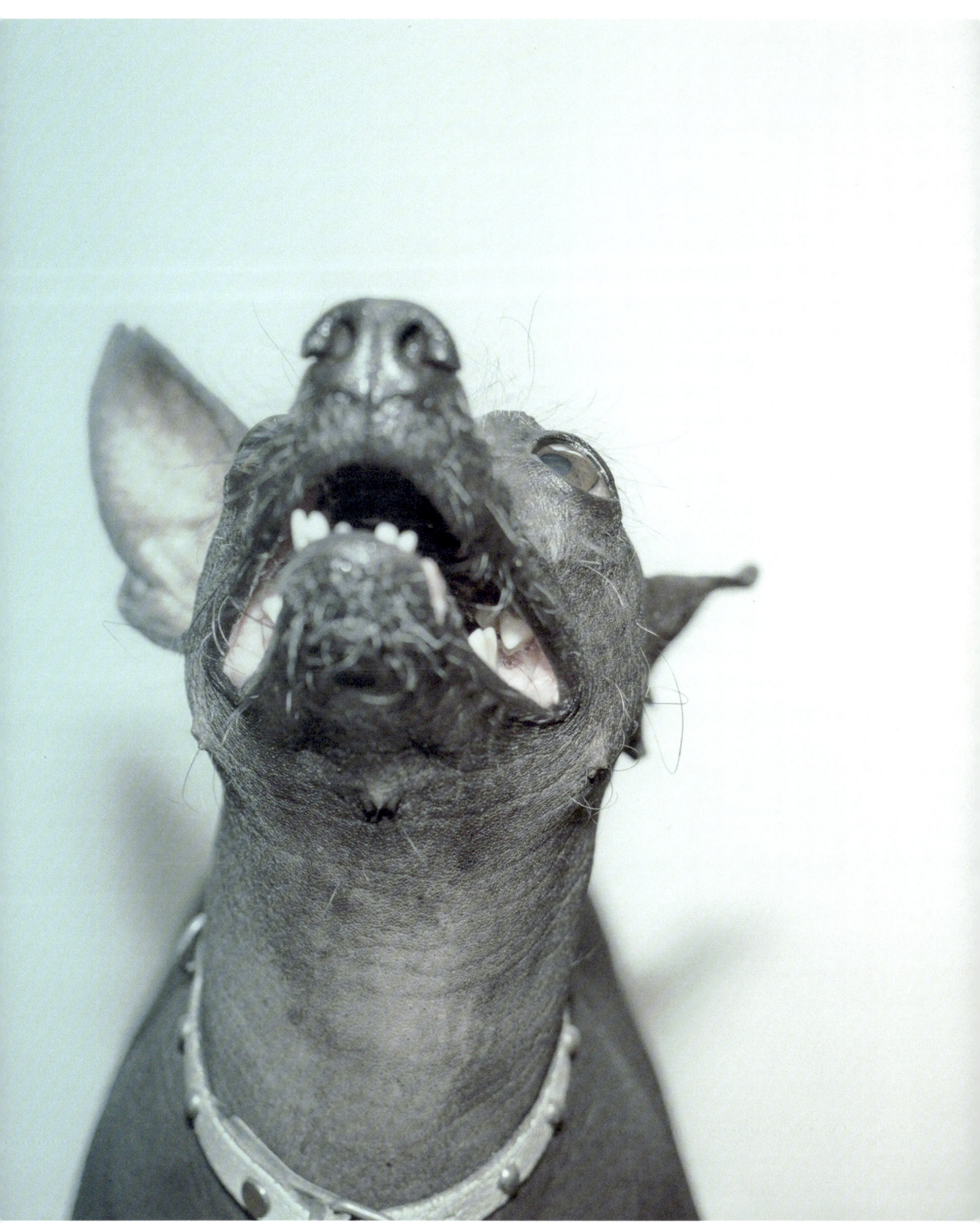

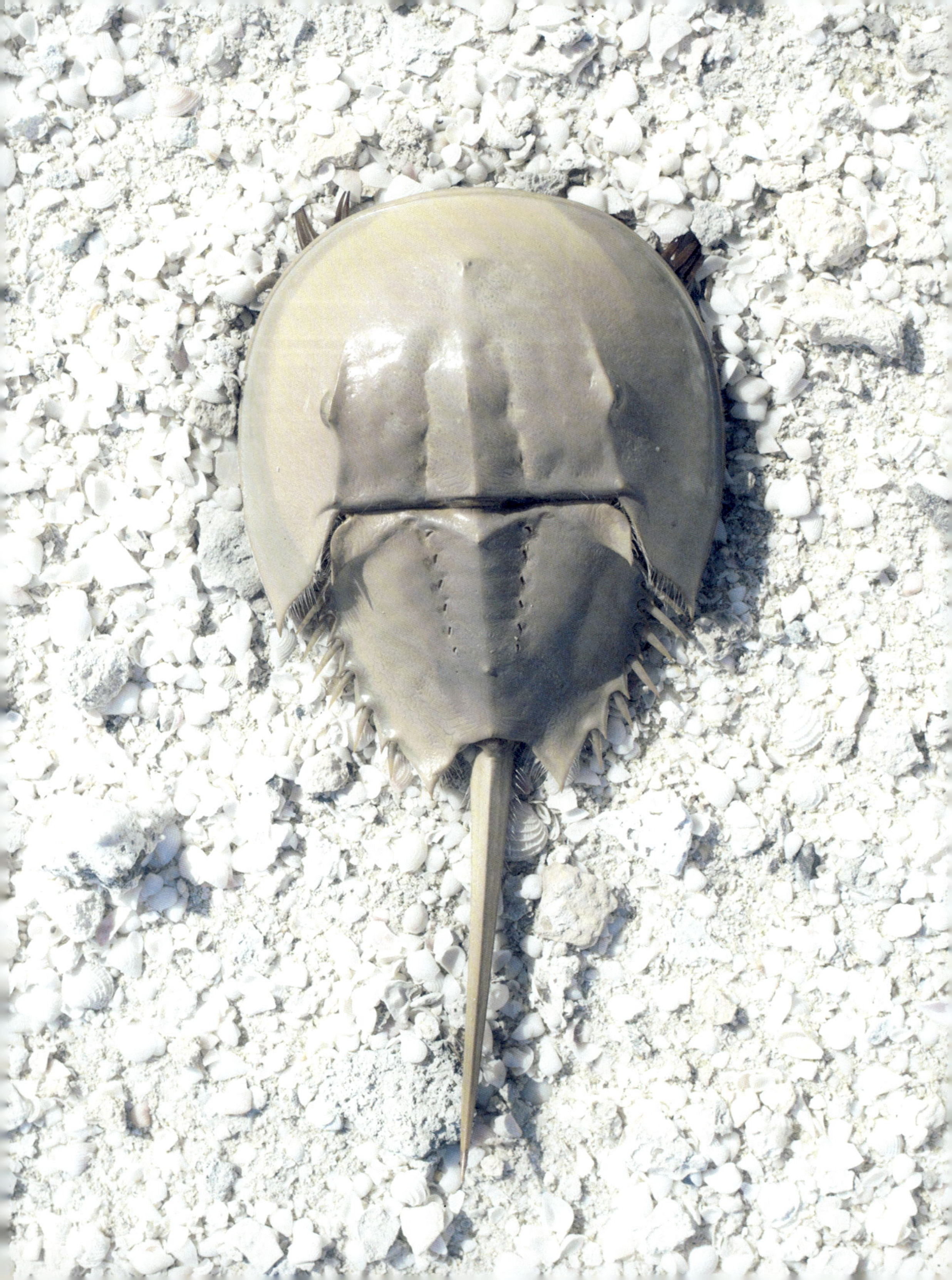

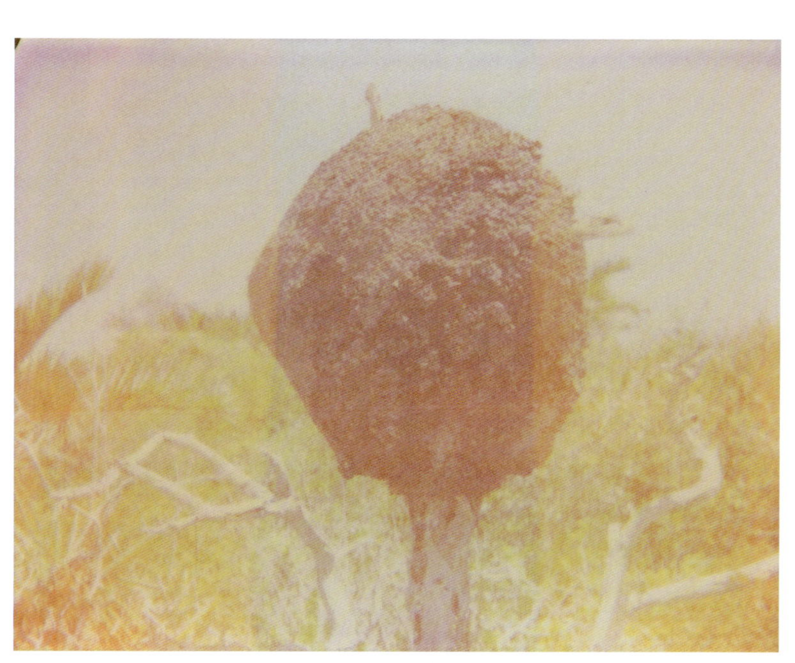

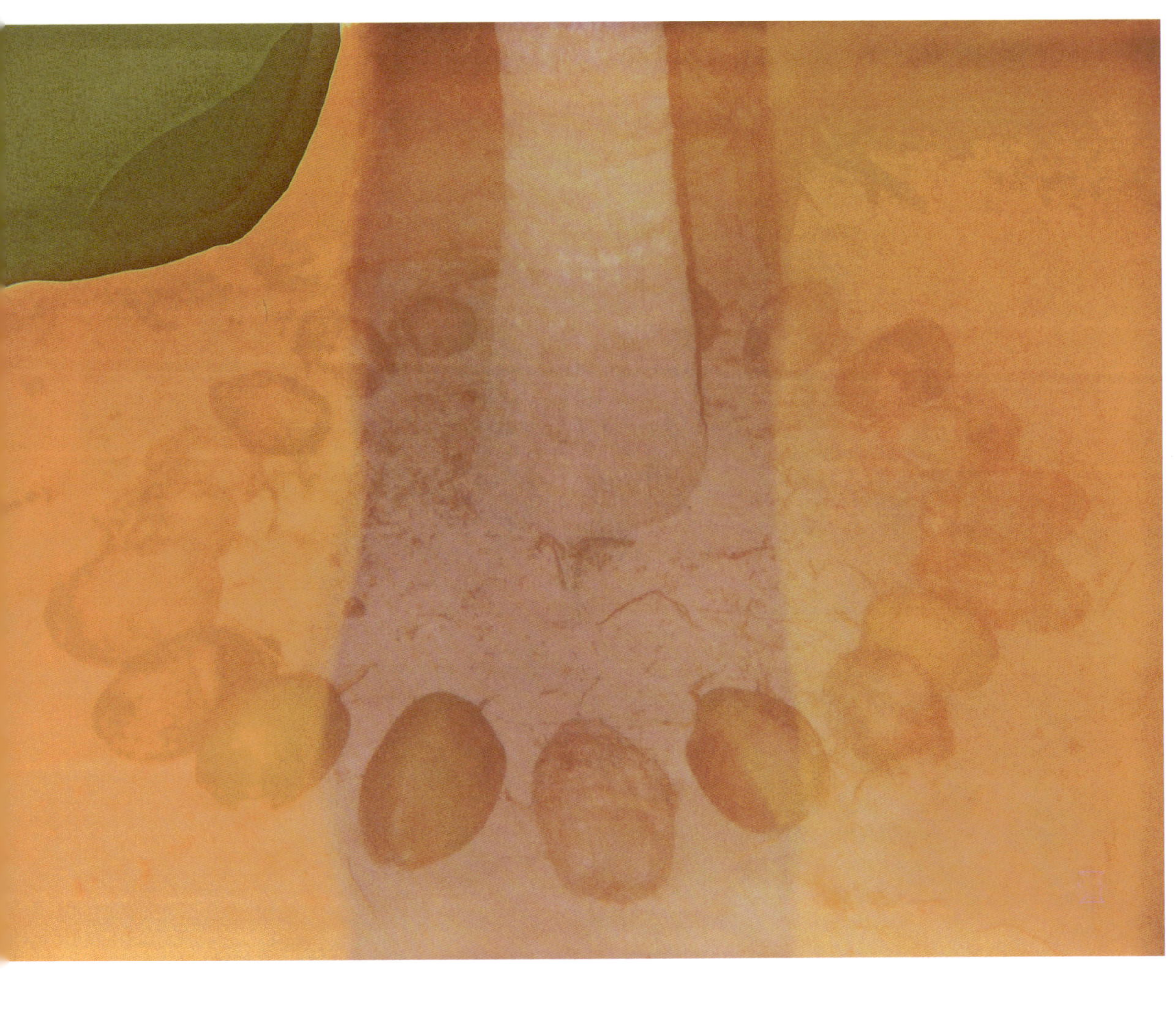

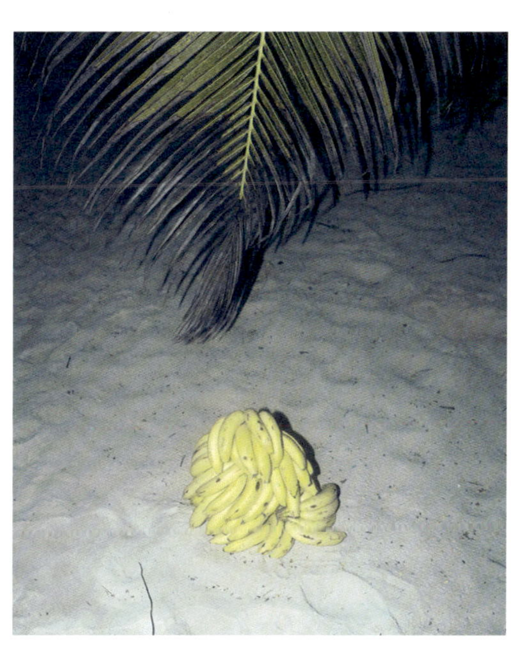

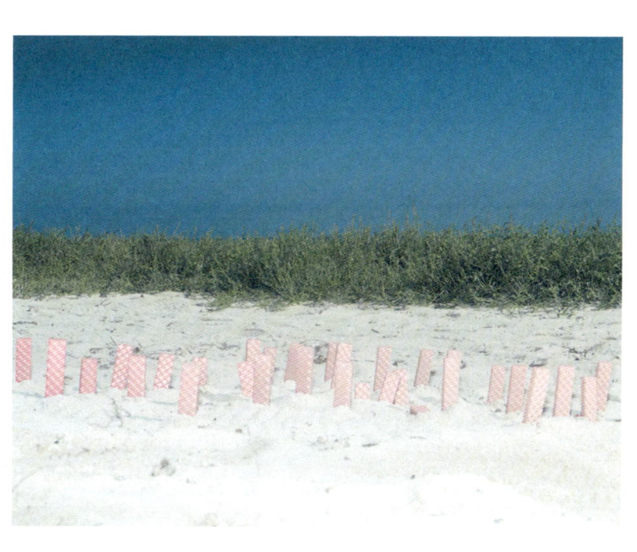

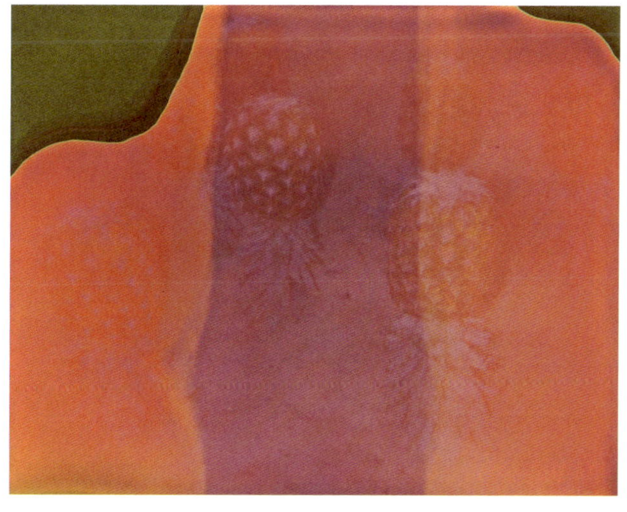

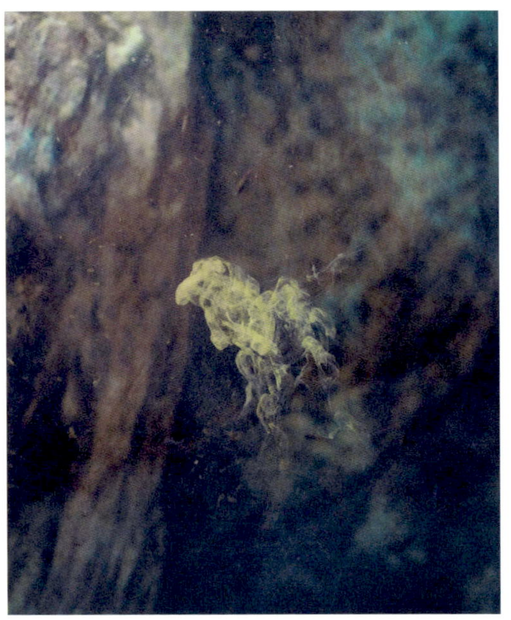

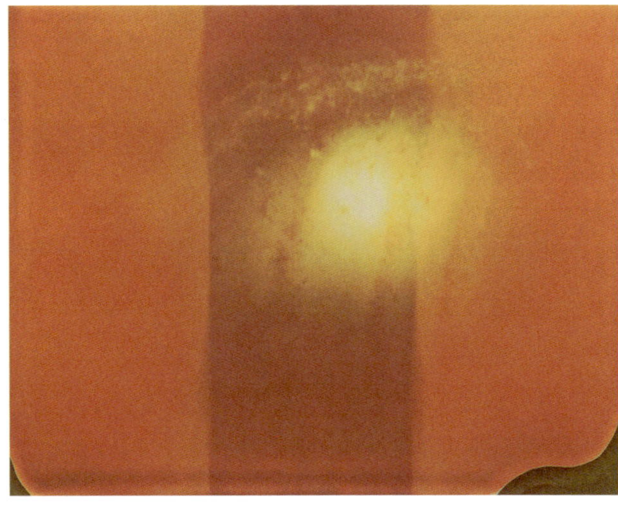

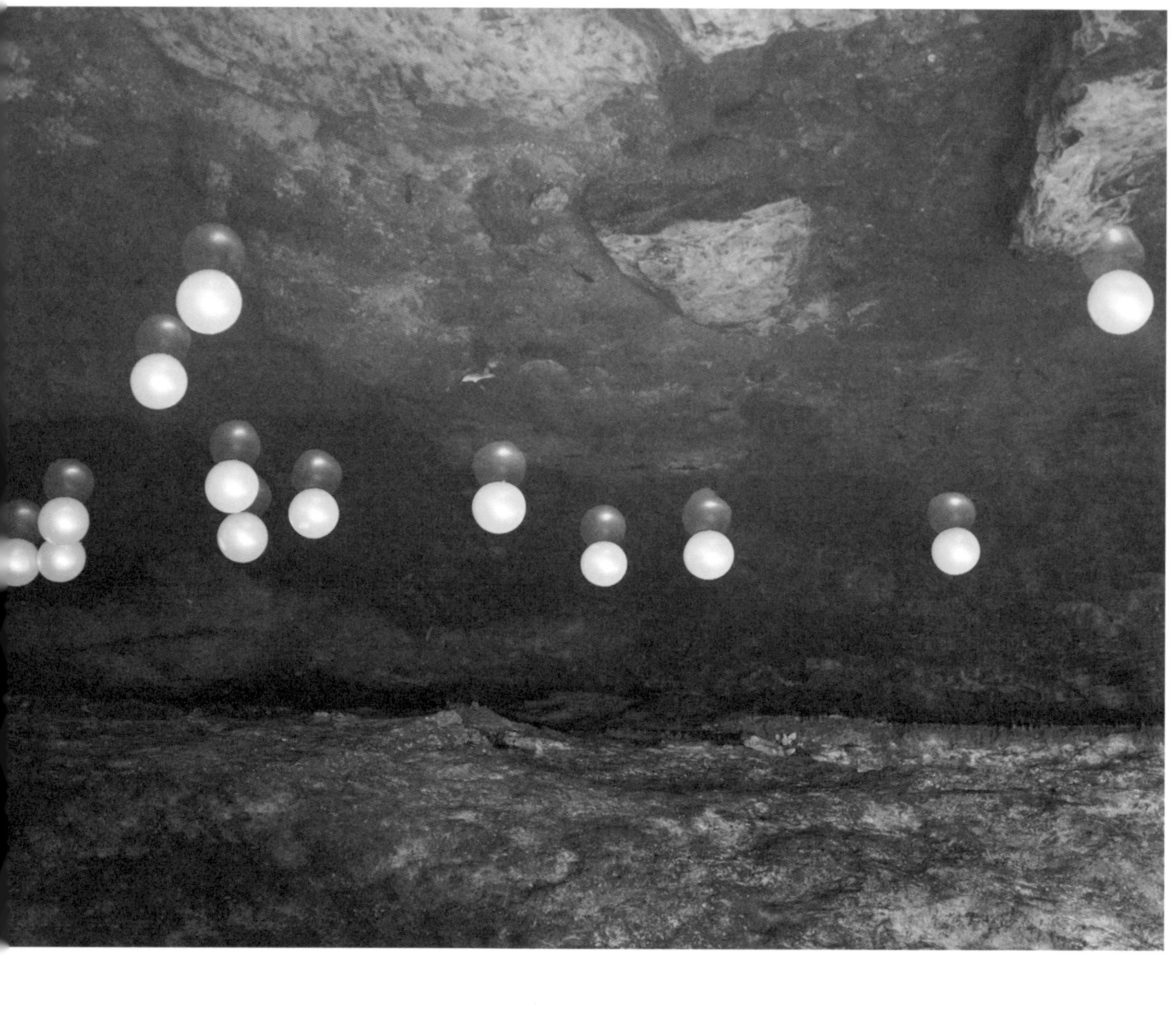

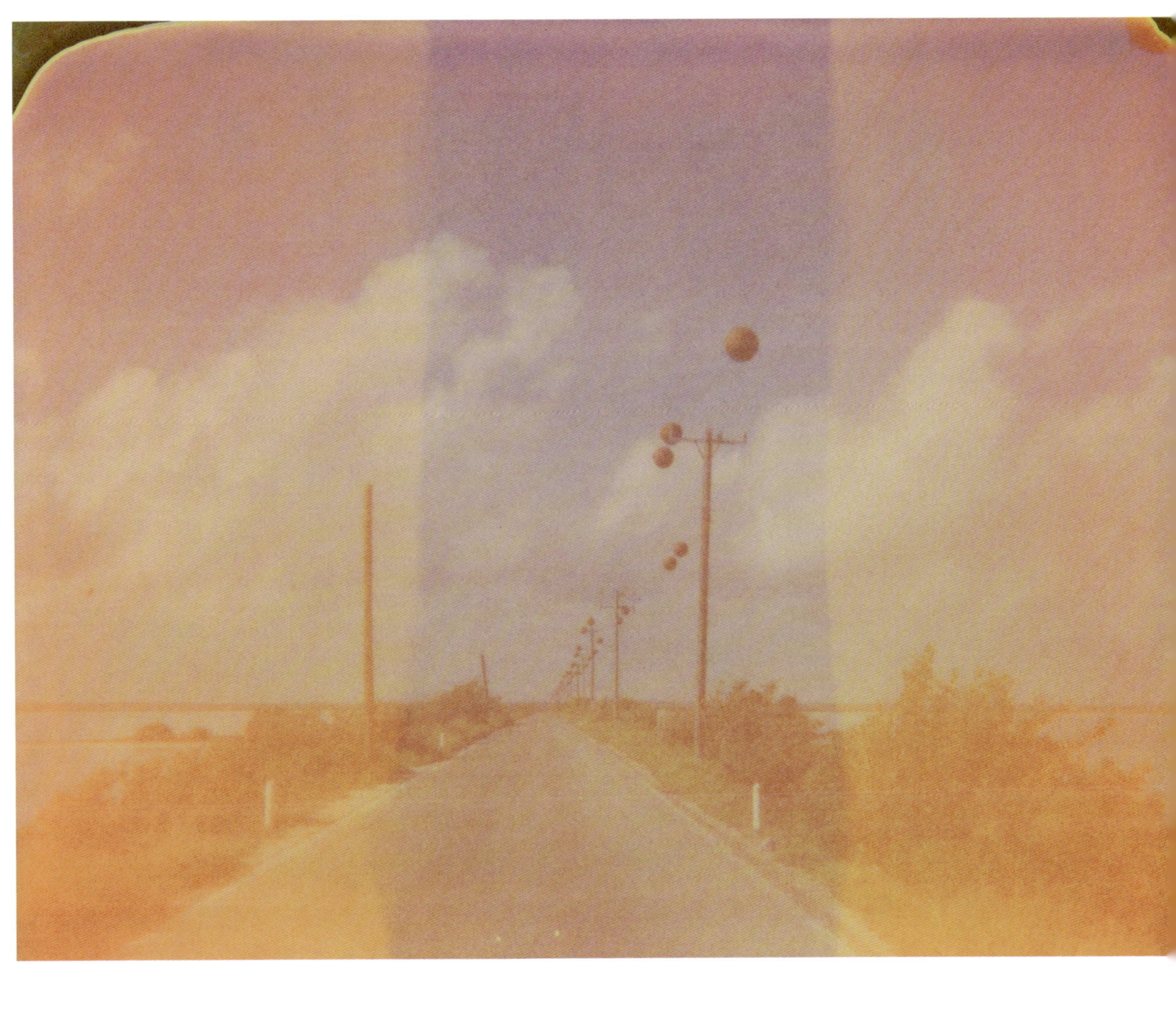

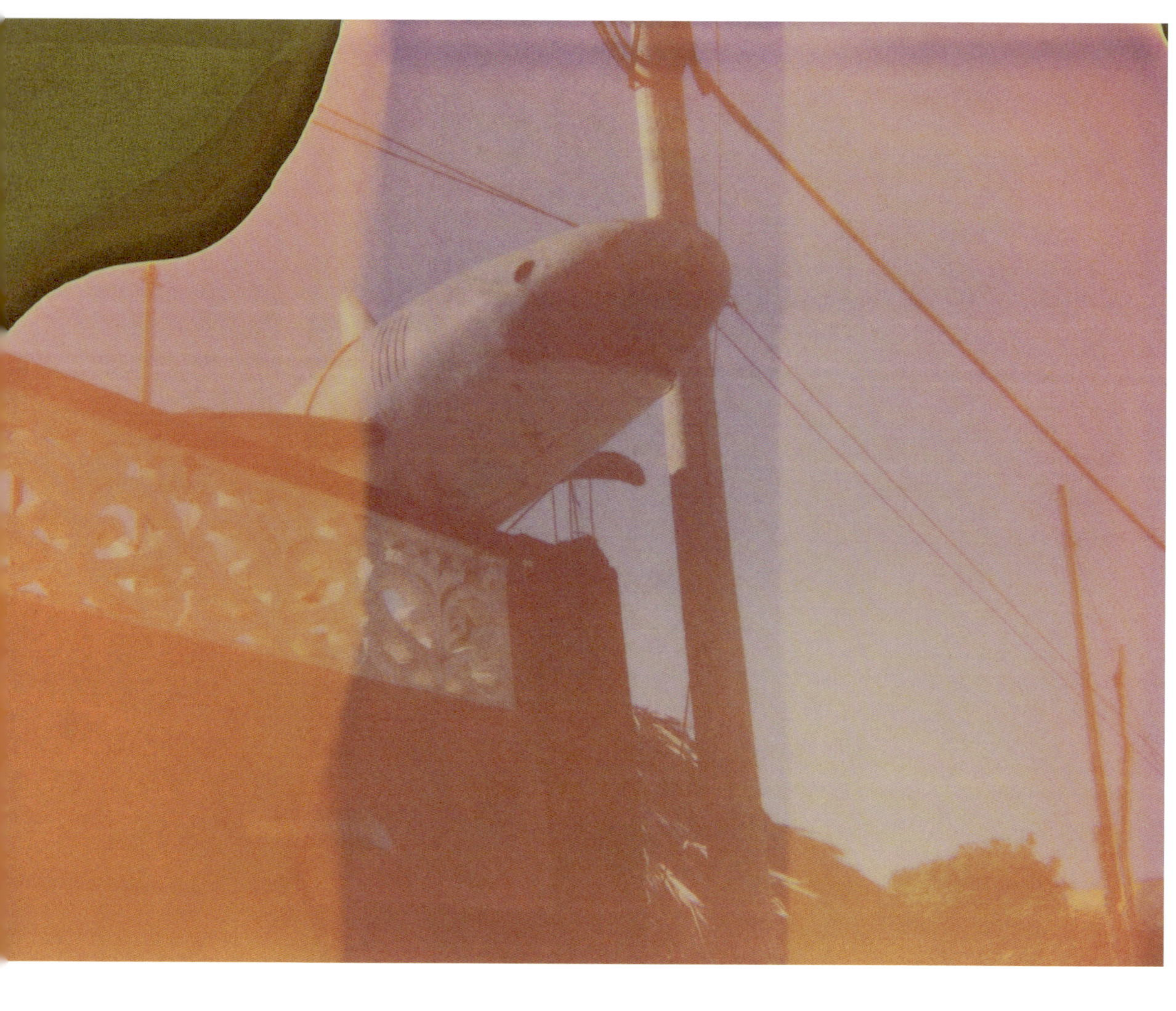

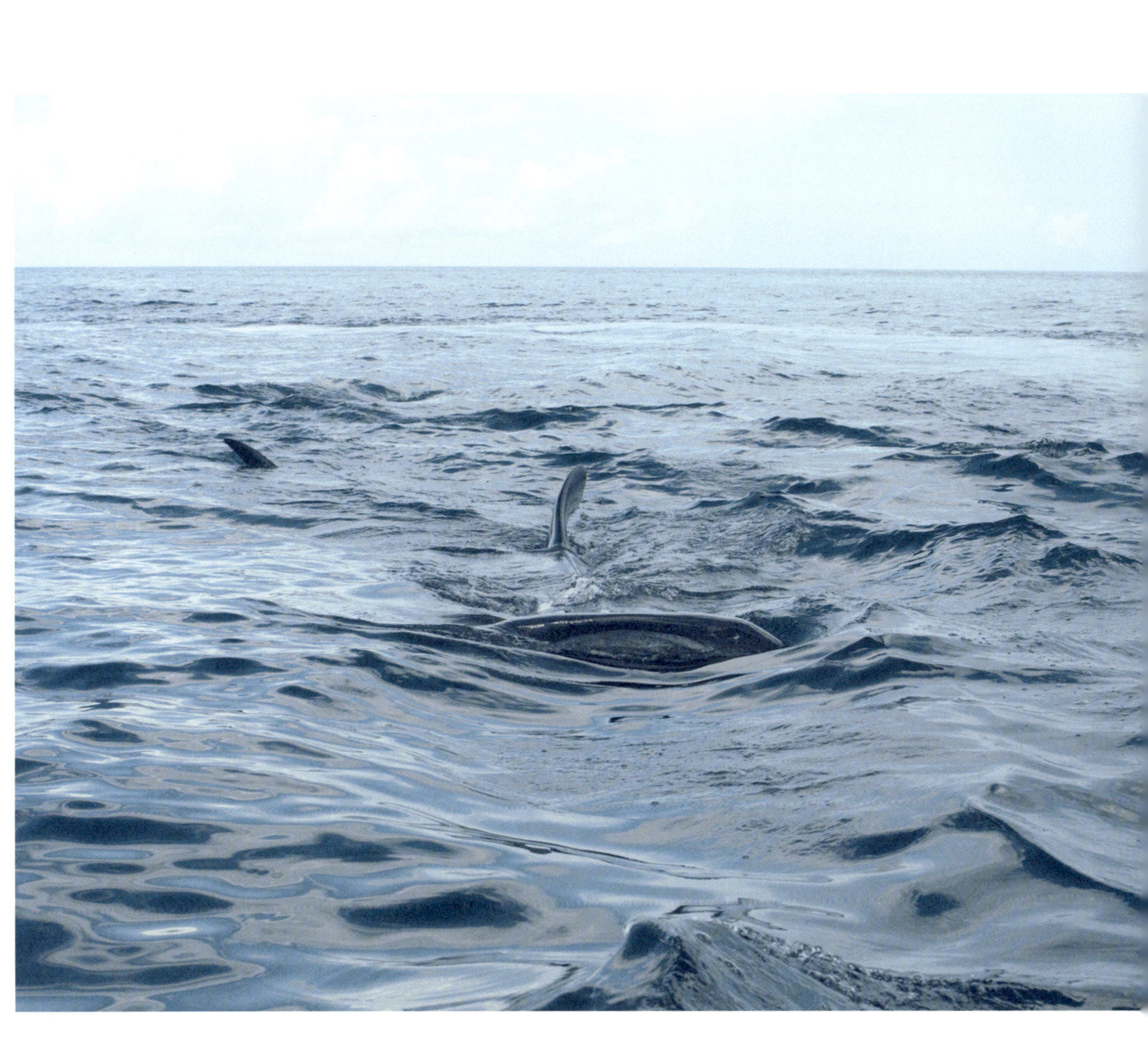

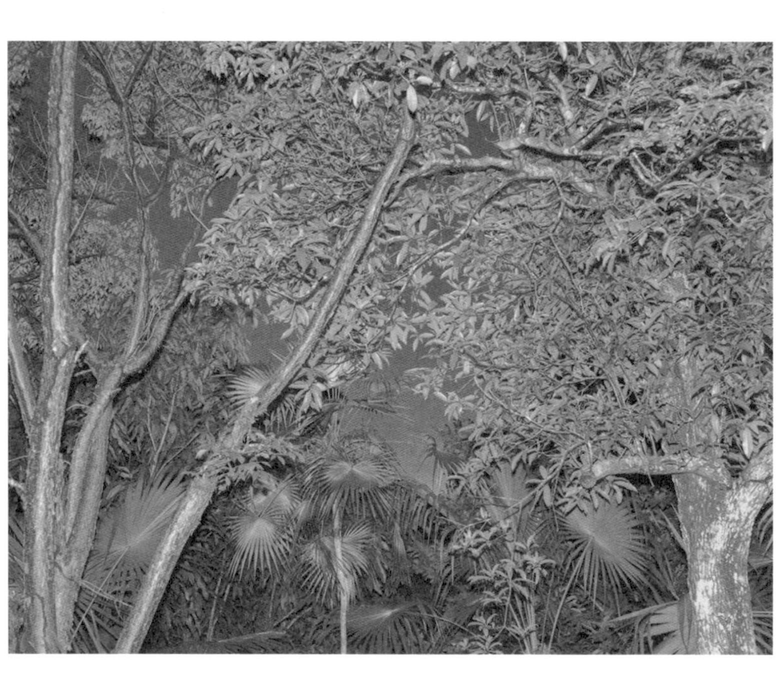

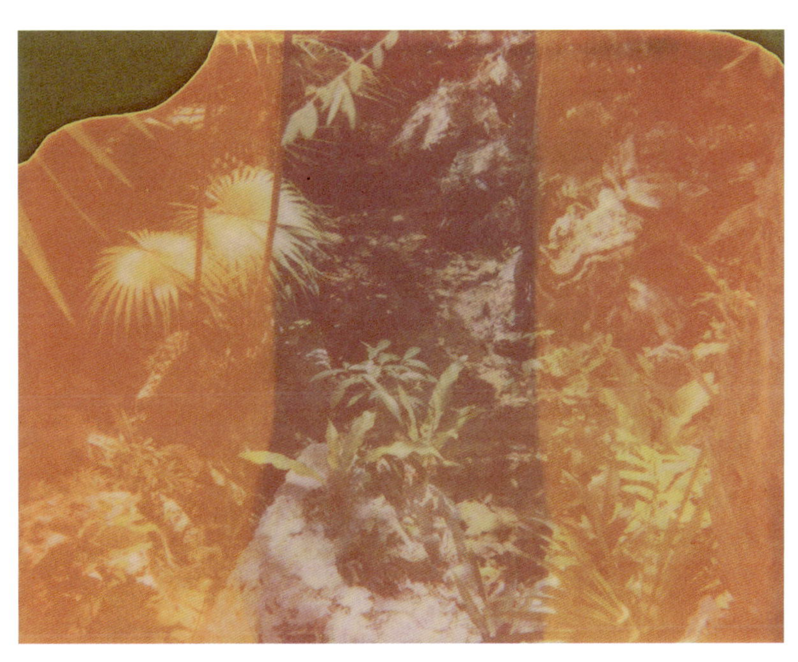

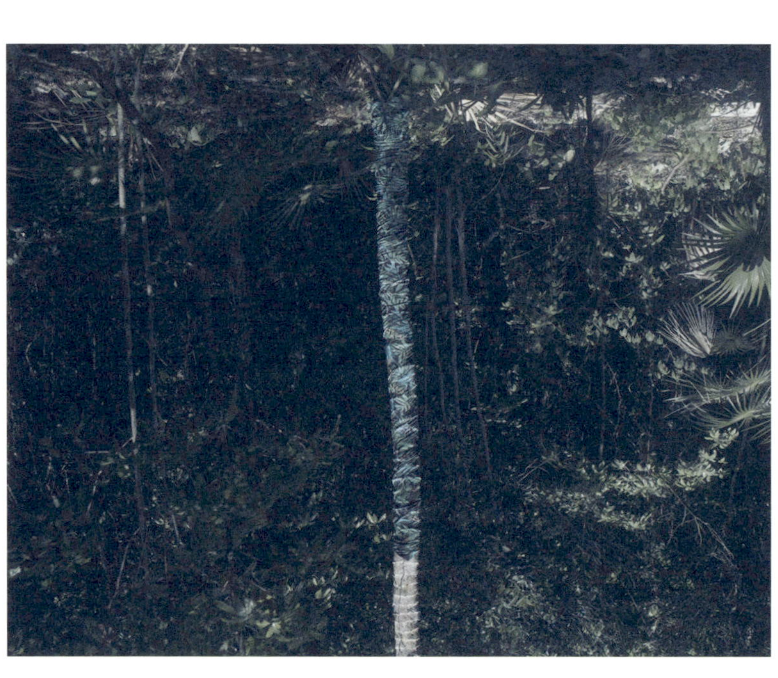

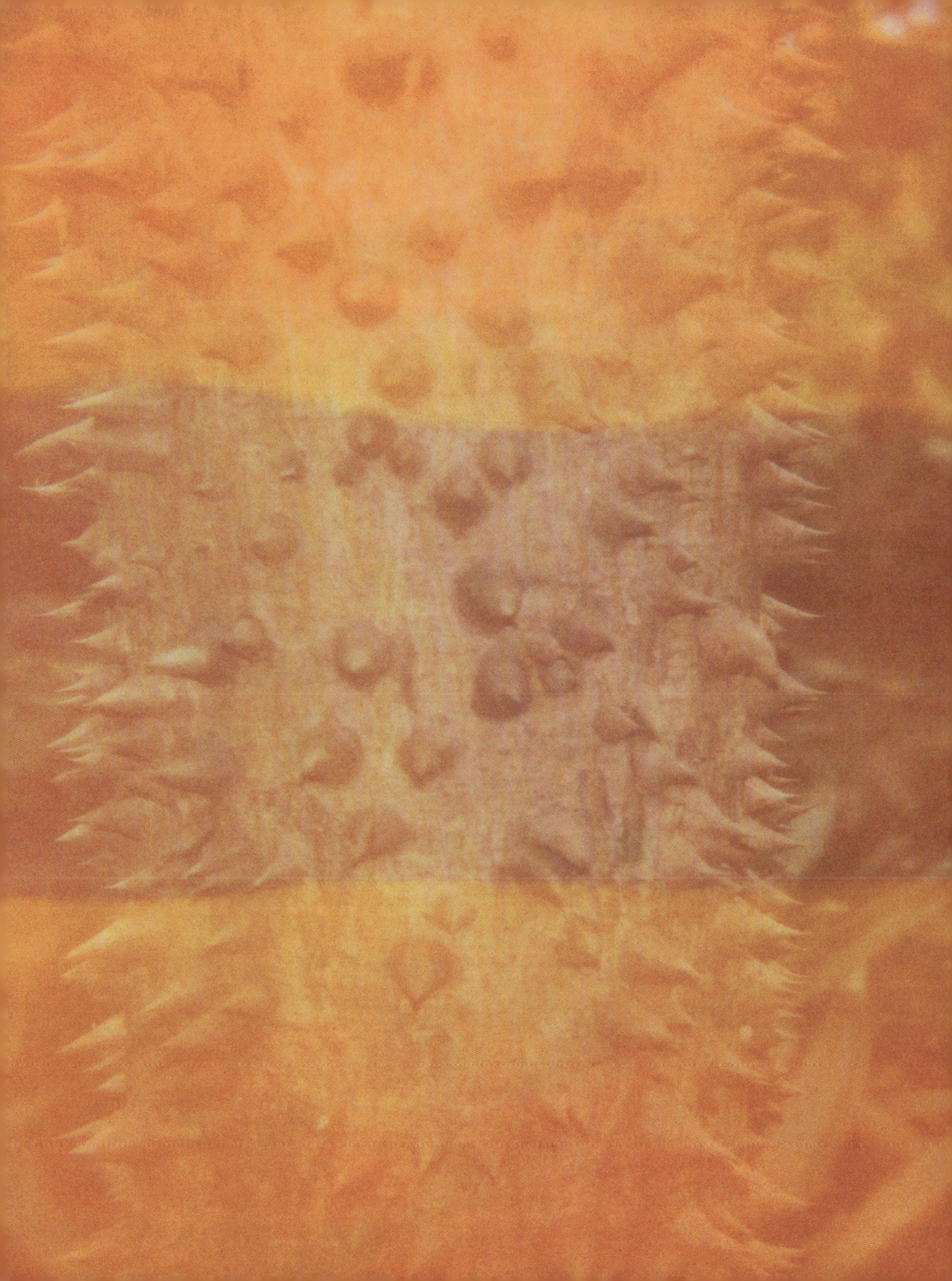

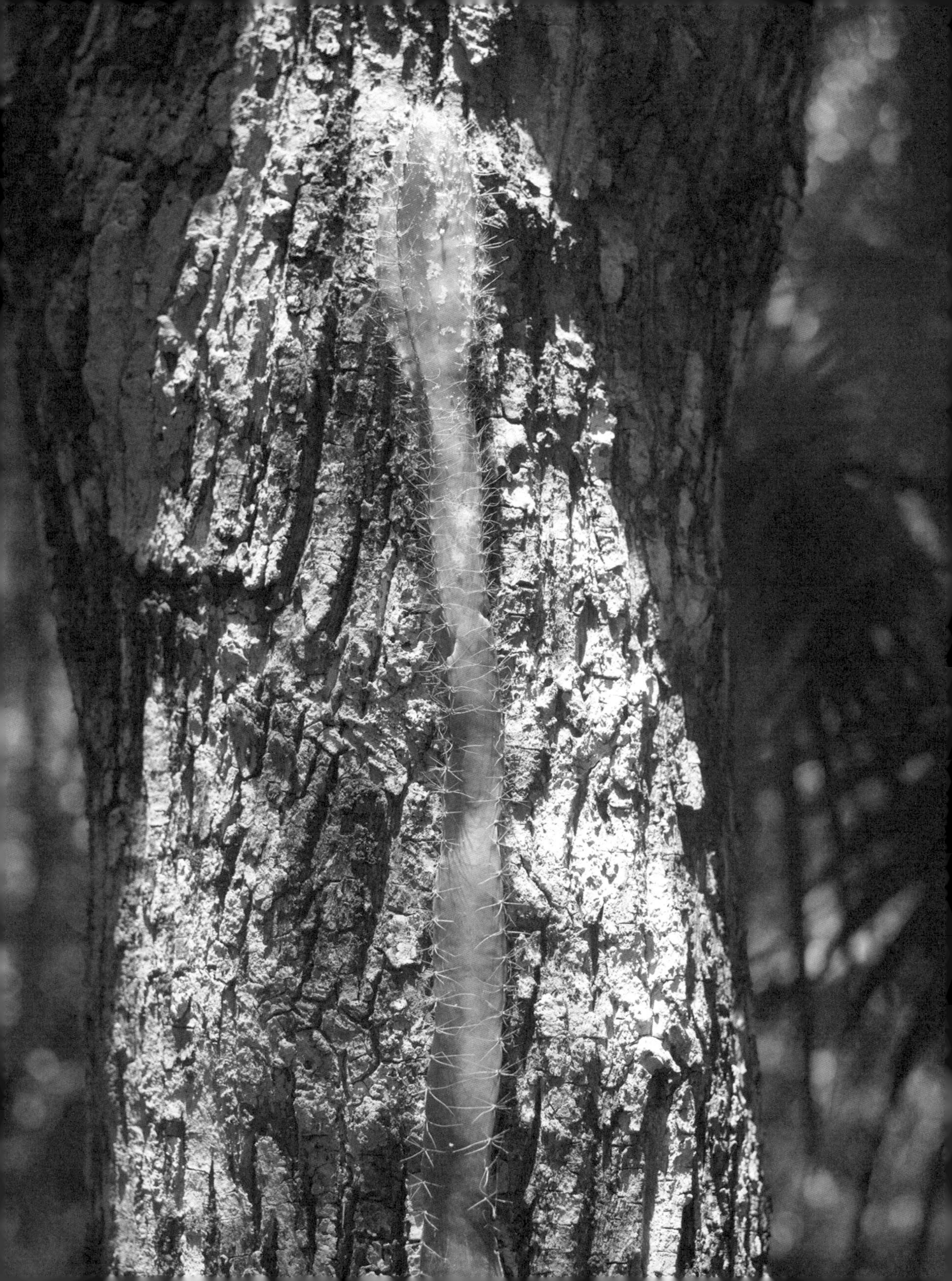

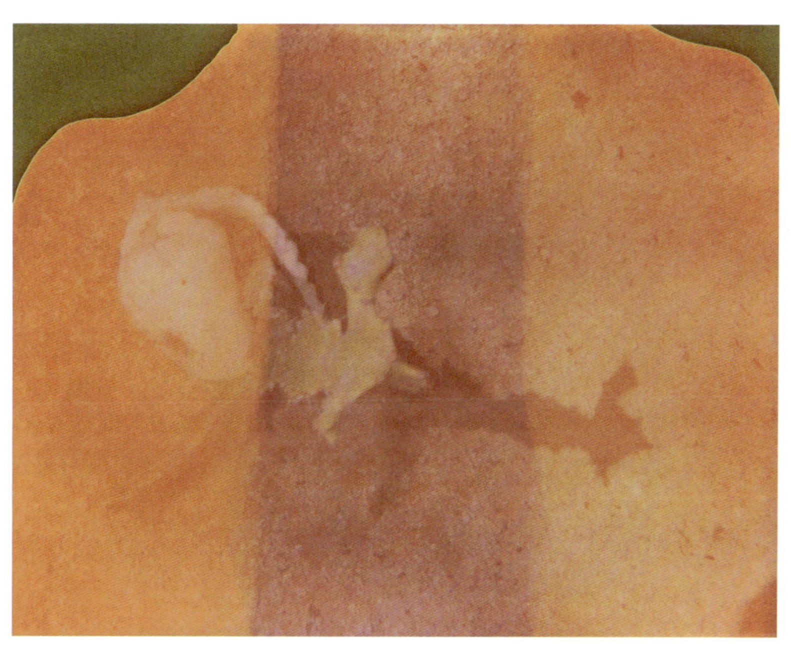

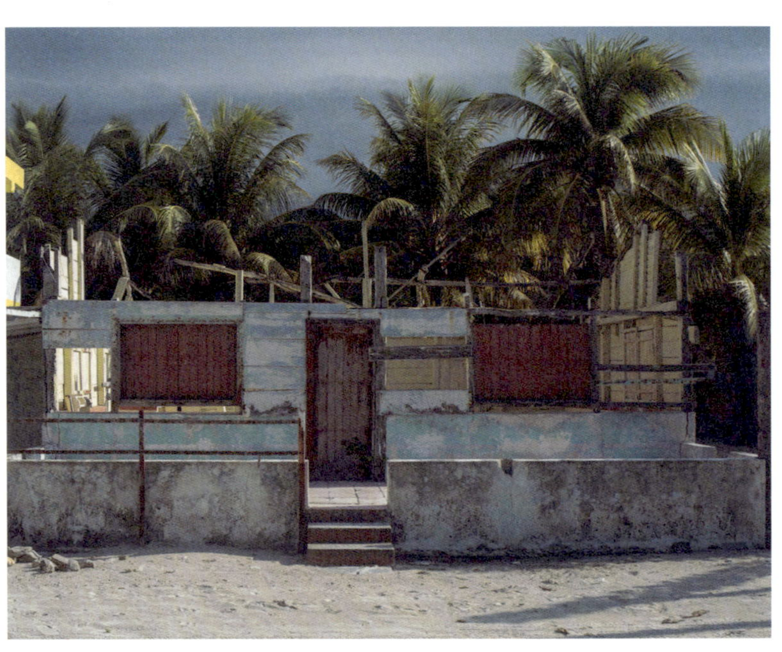

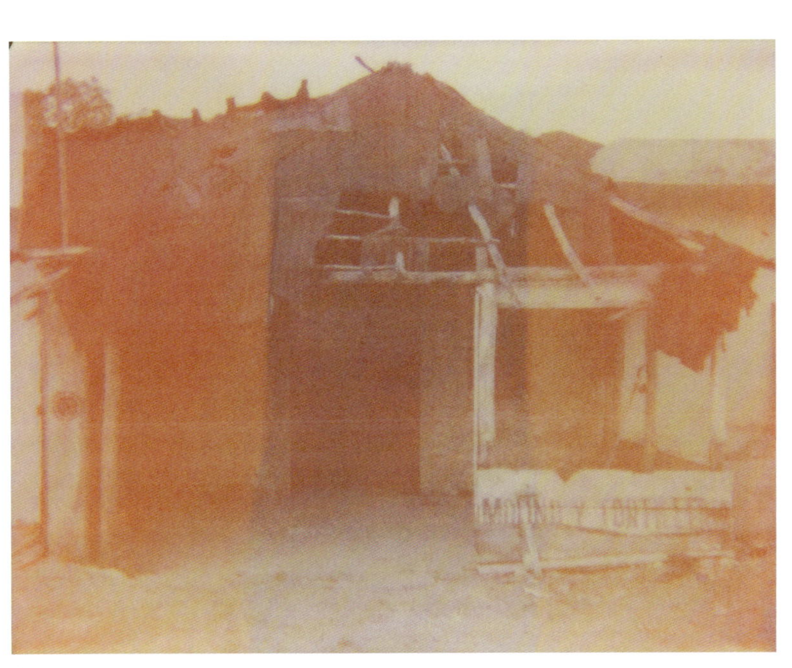

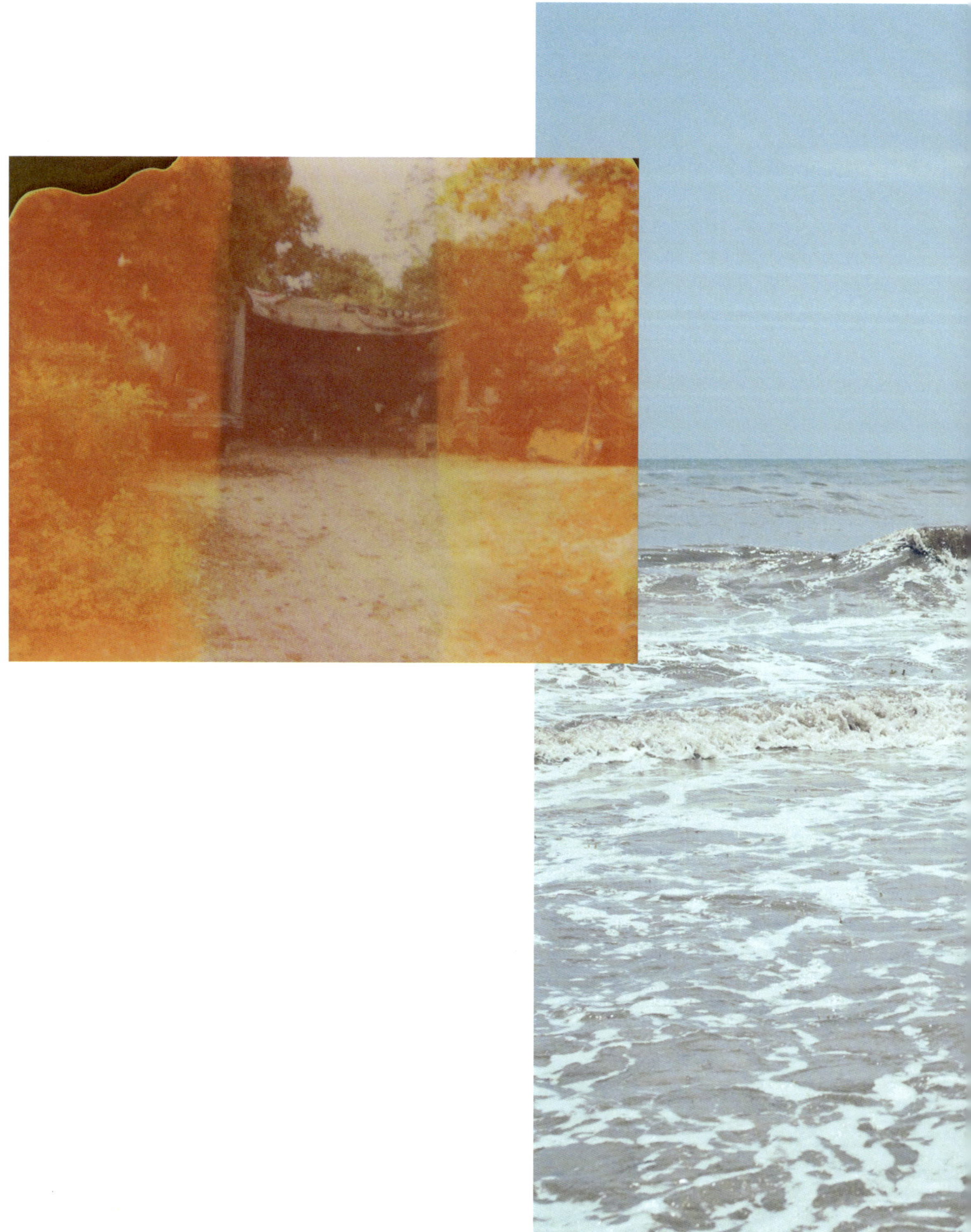

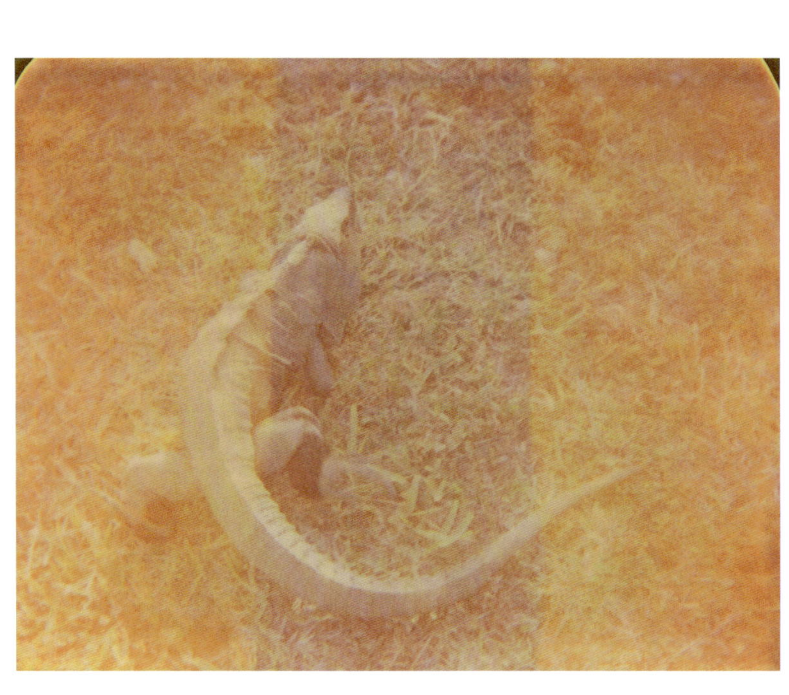

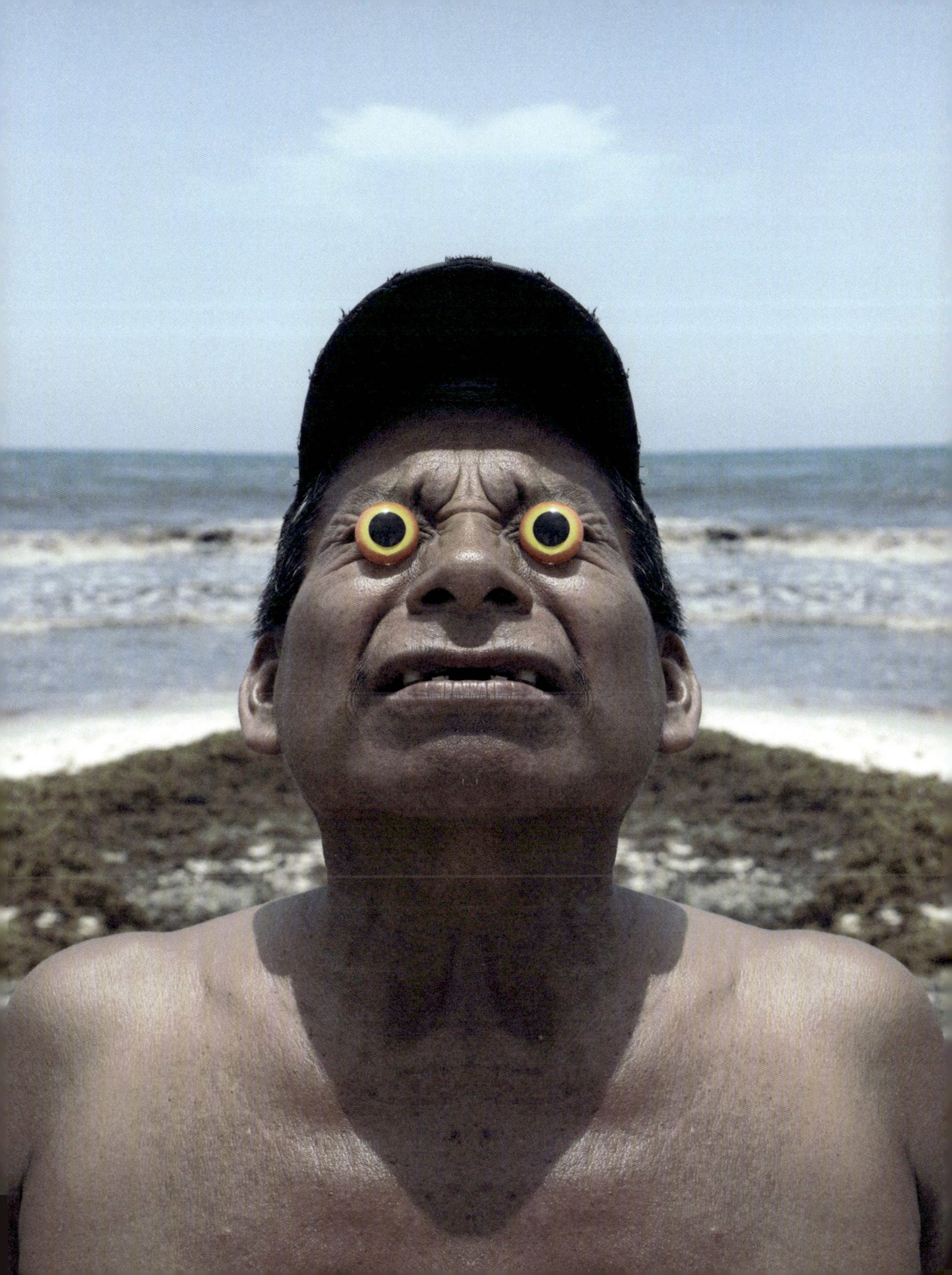

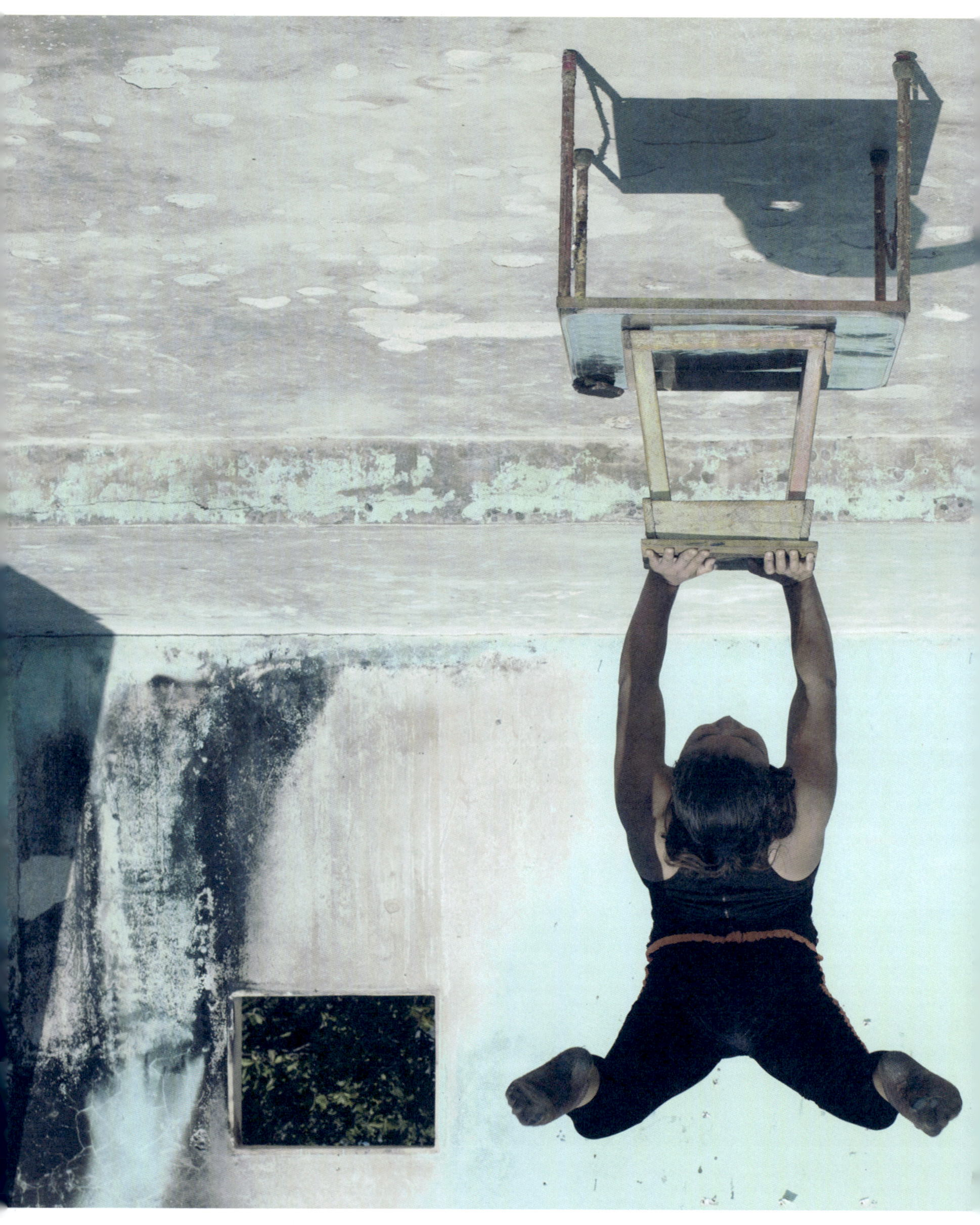

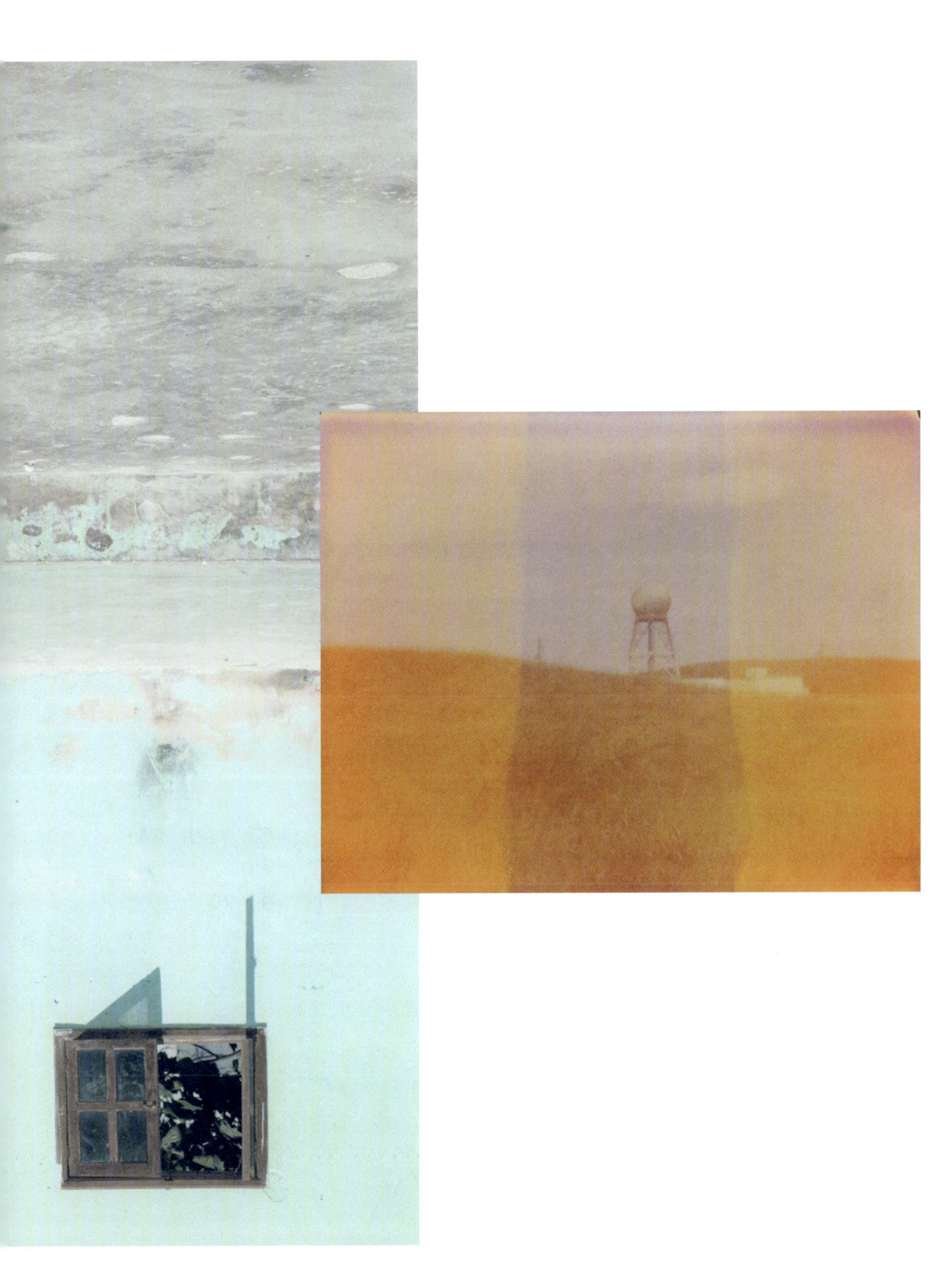

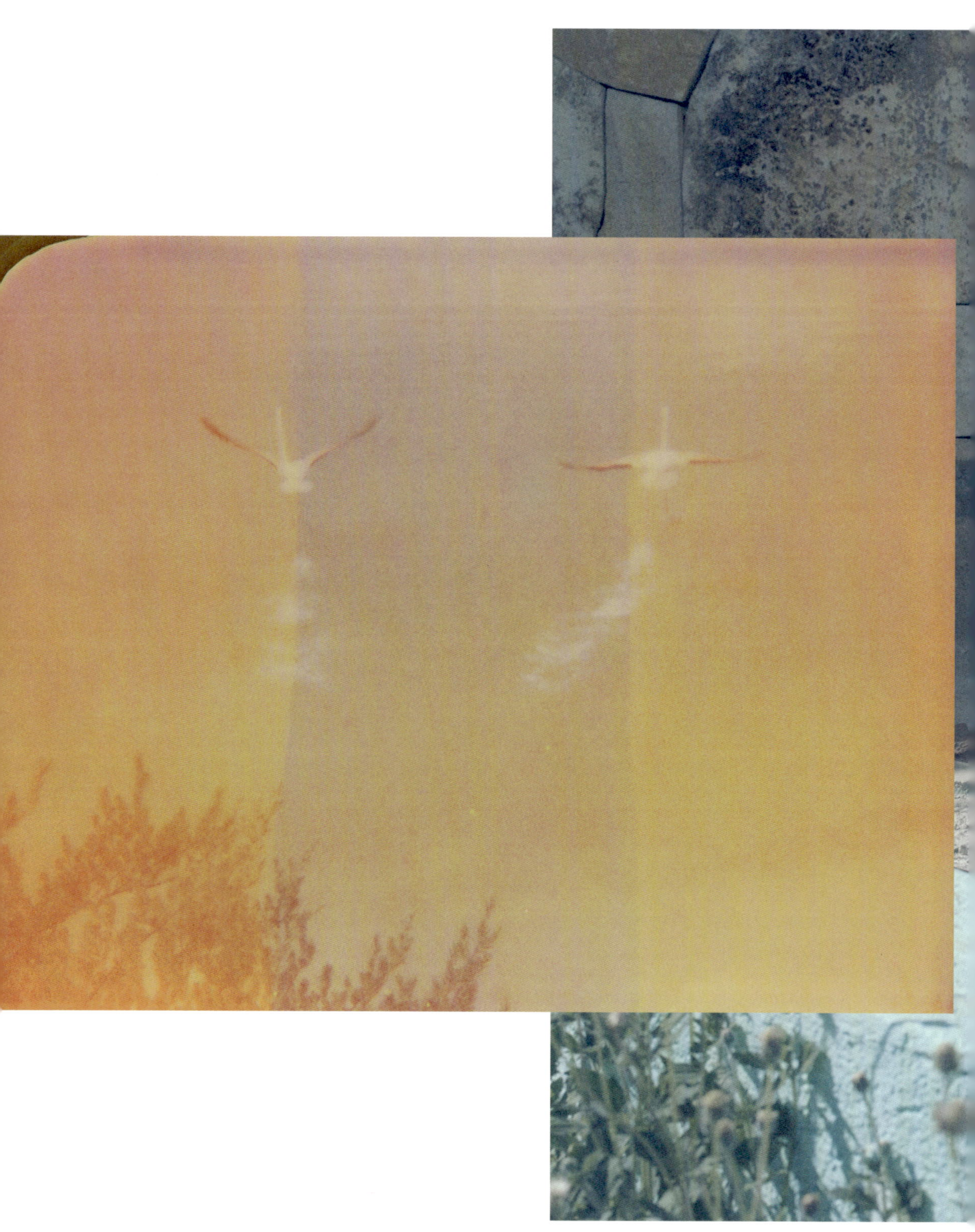

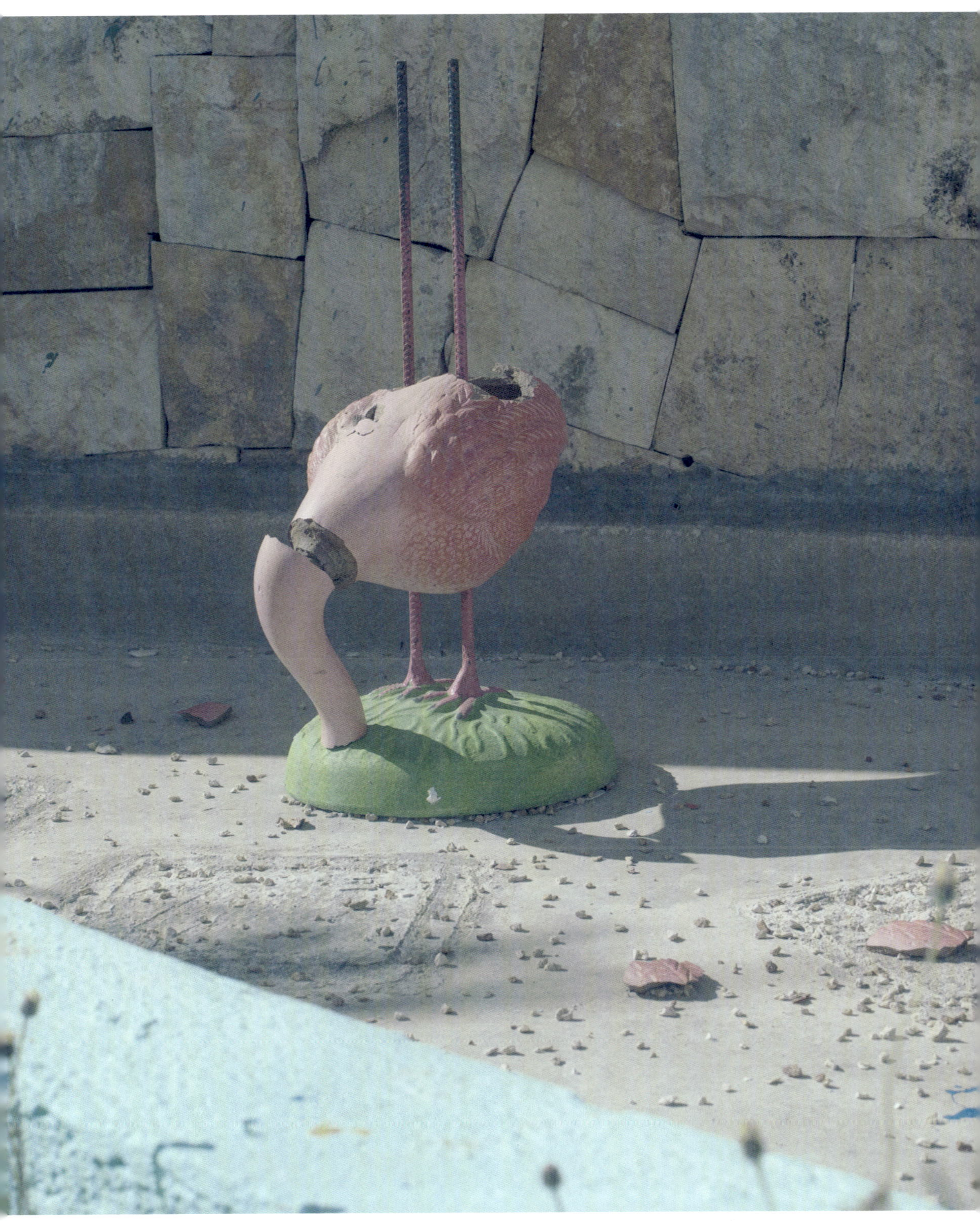

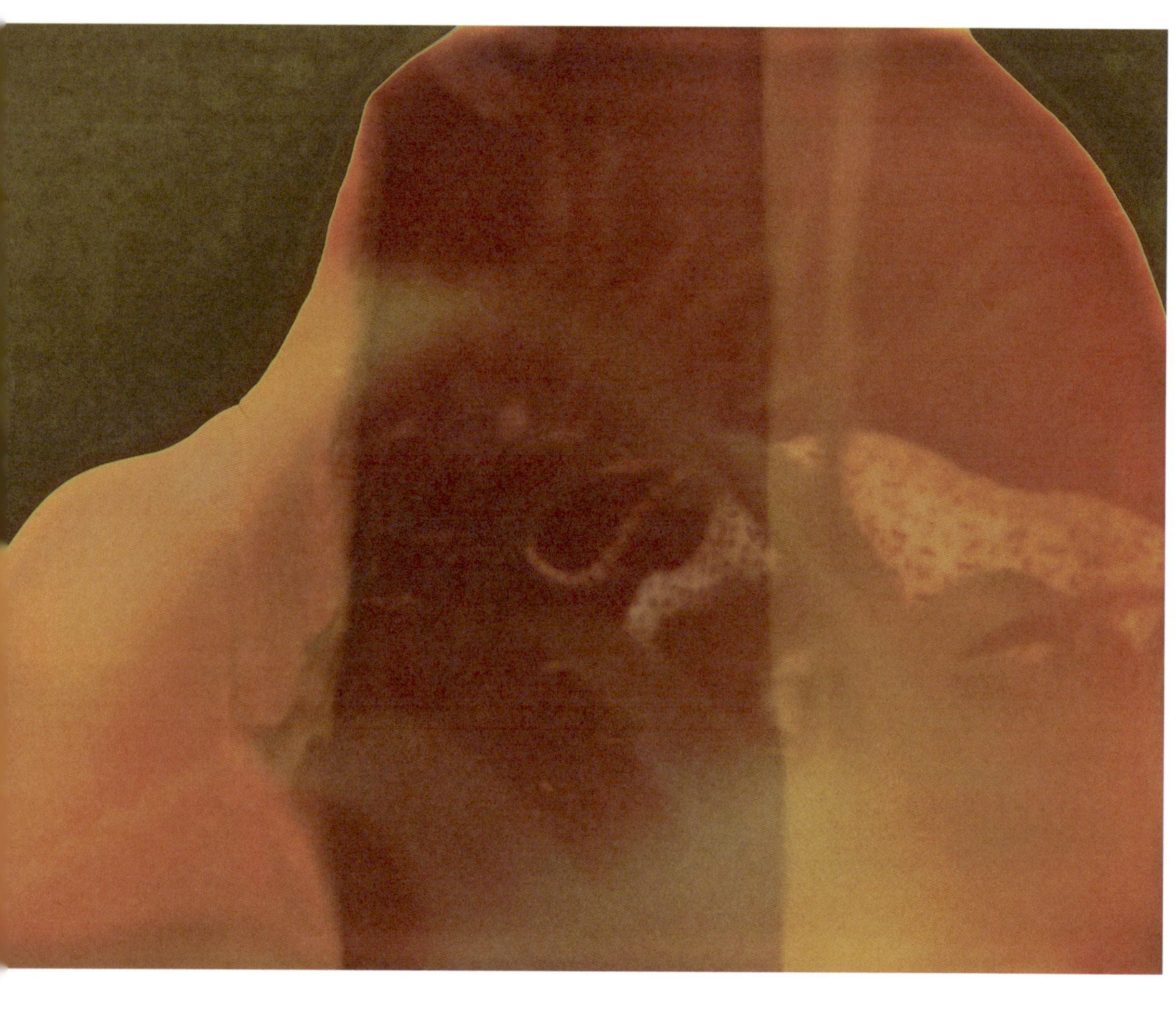

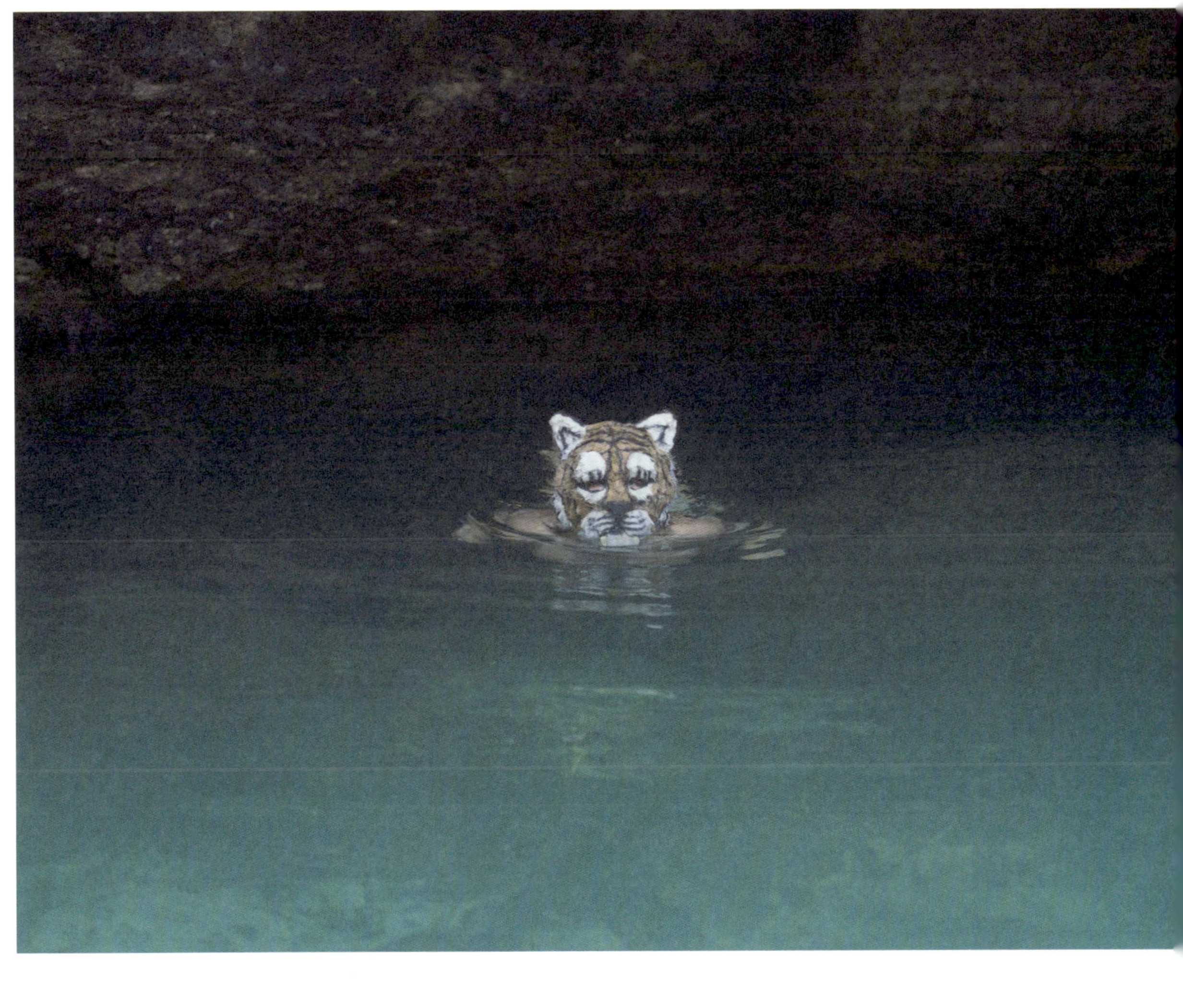

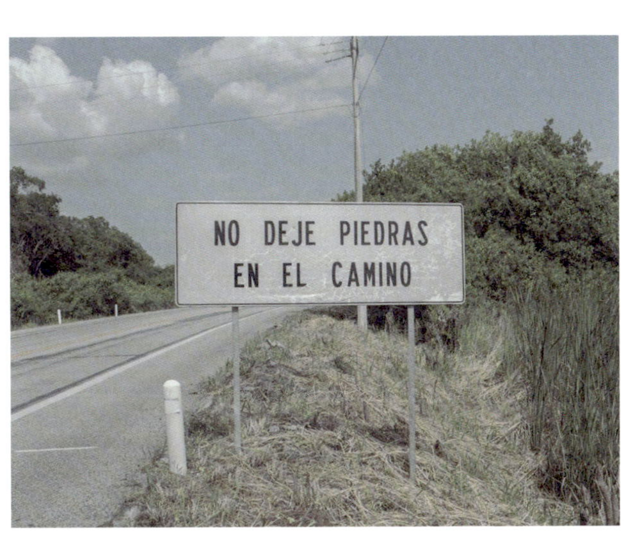
NO DEJE PIEDRAS
EN EL CAMINO

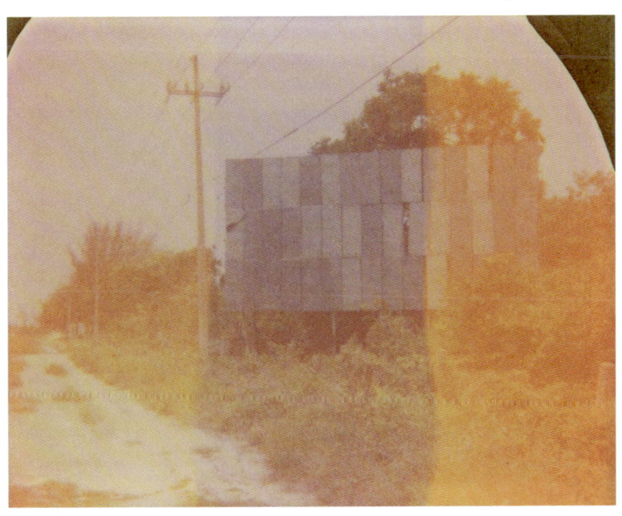

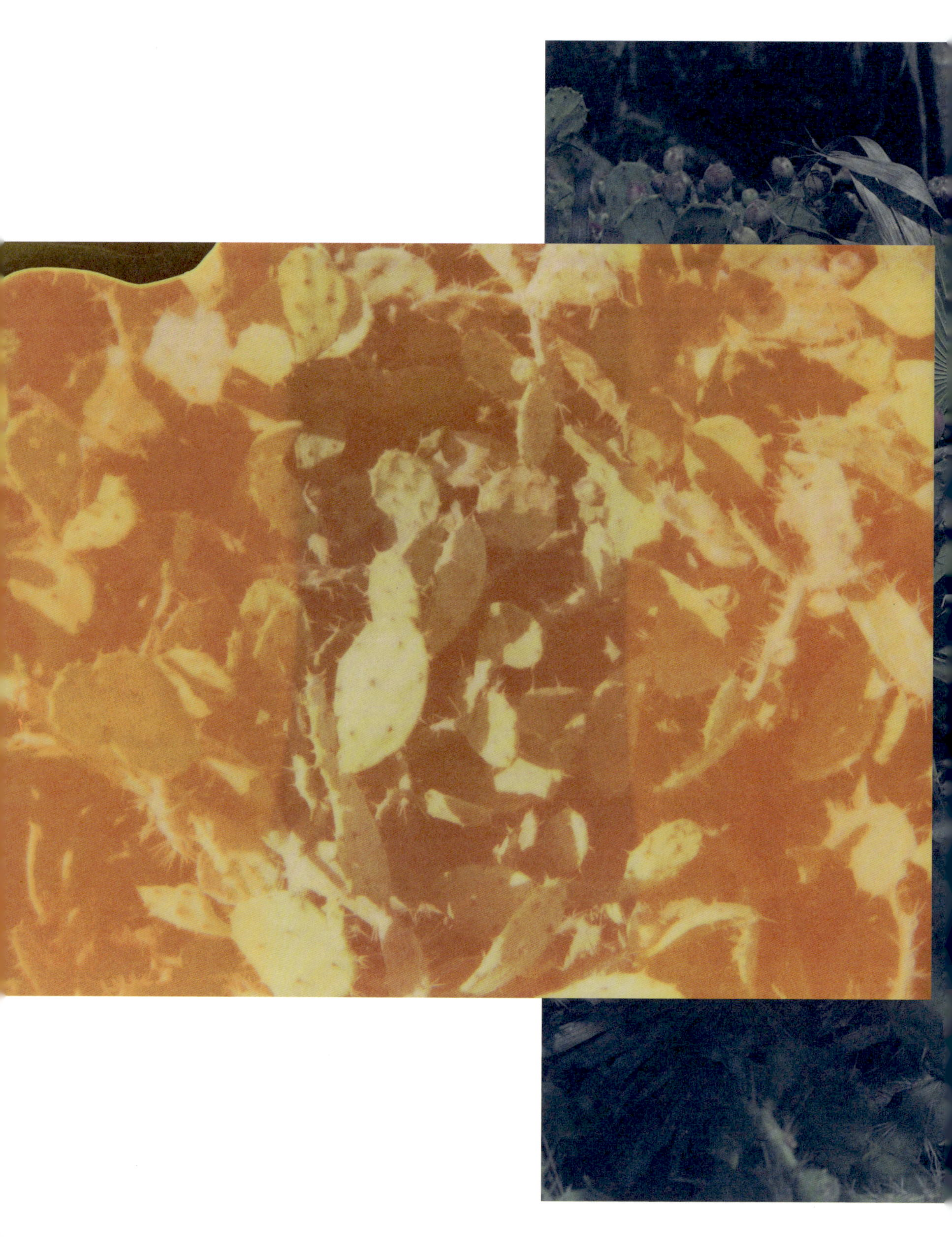

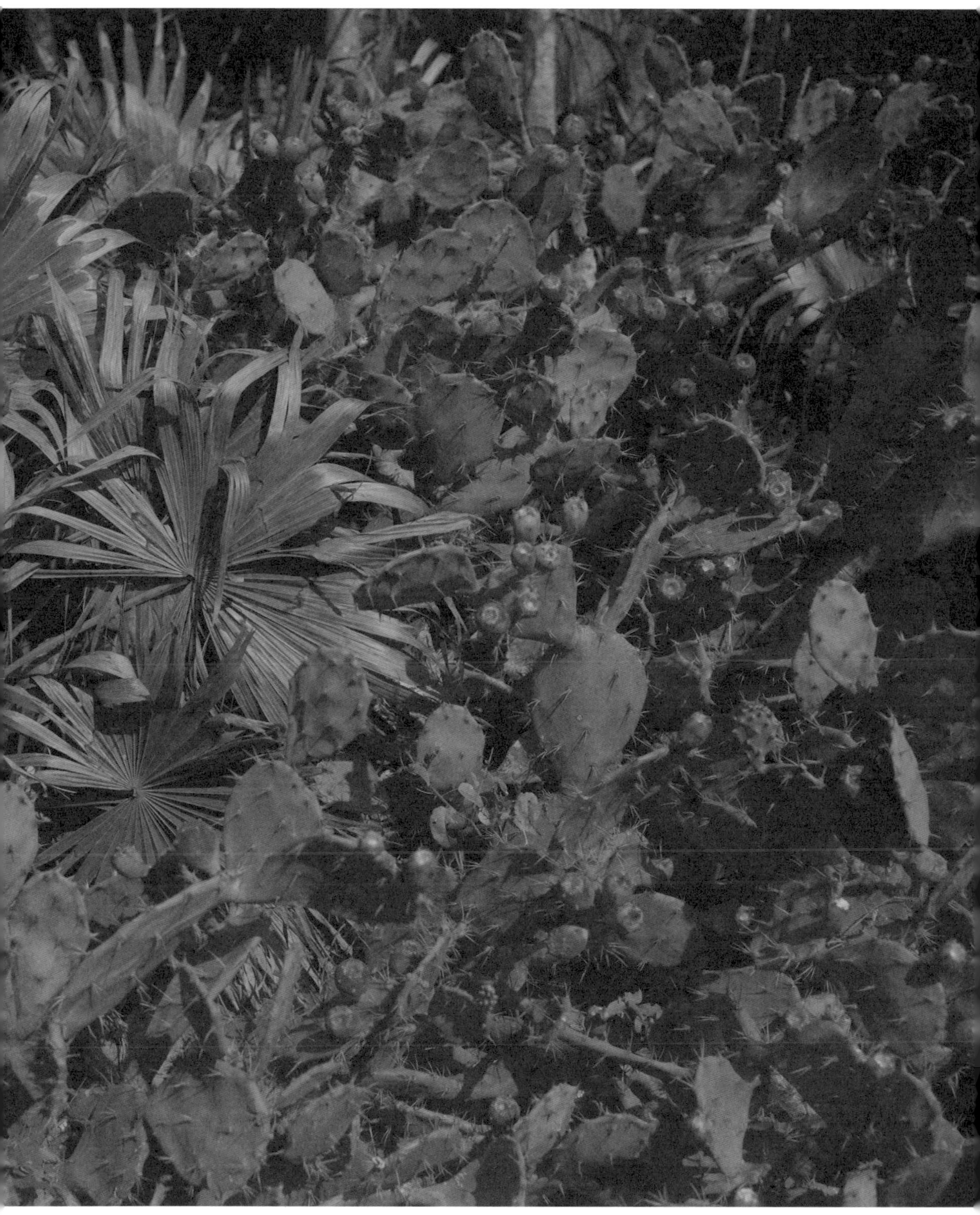

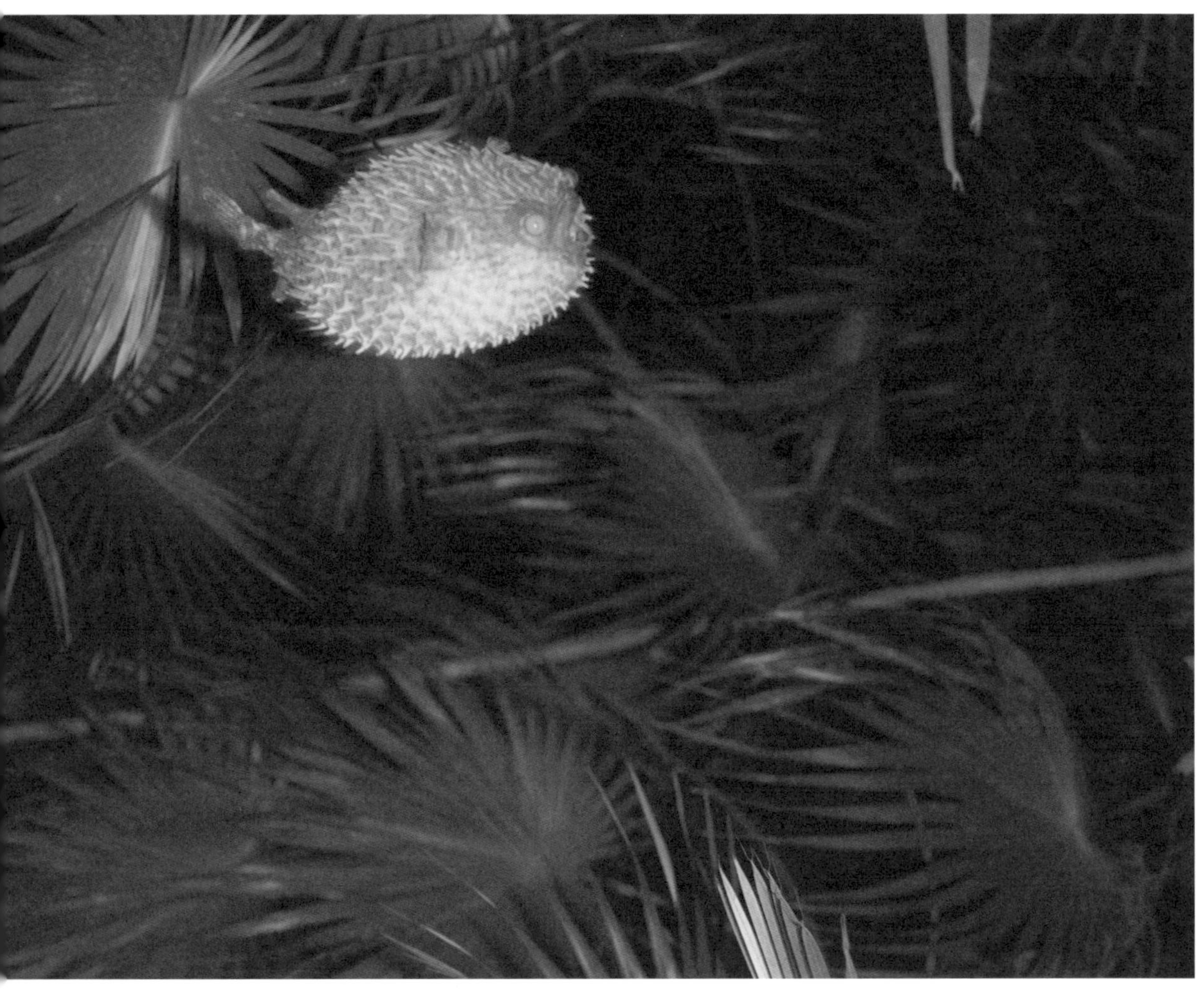

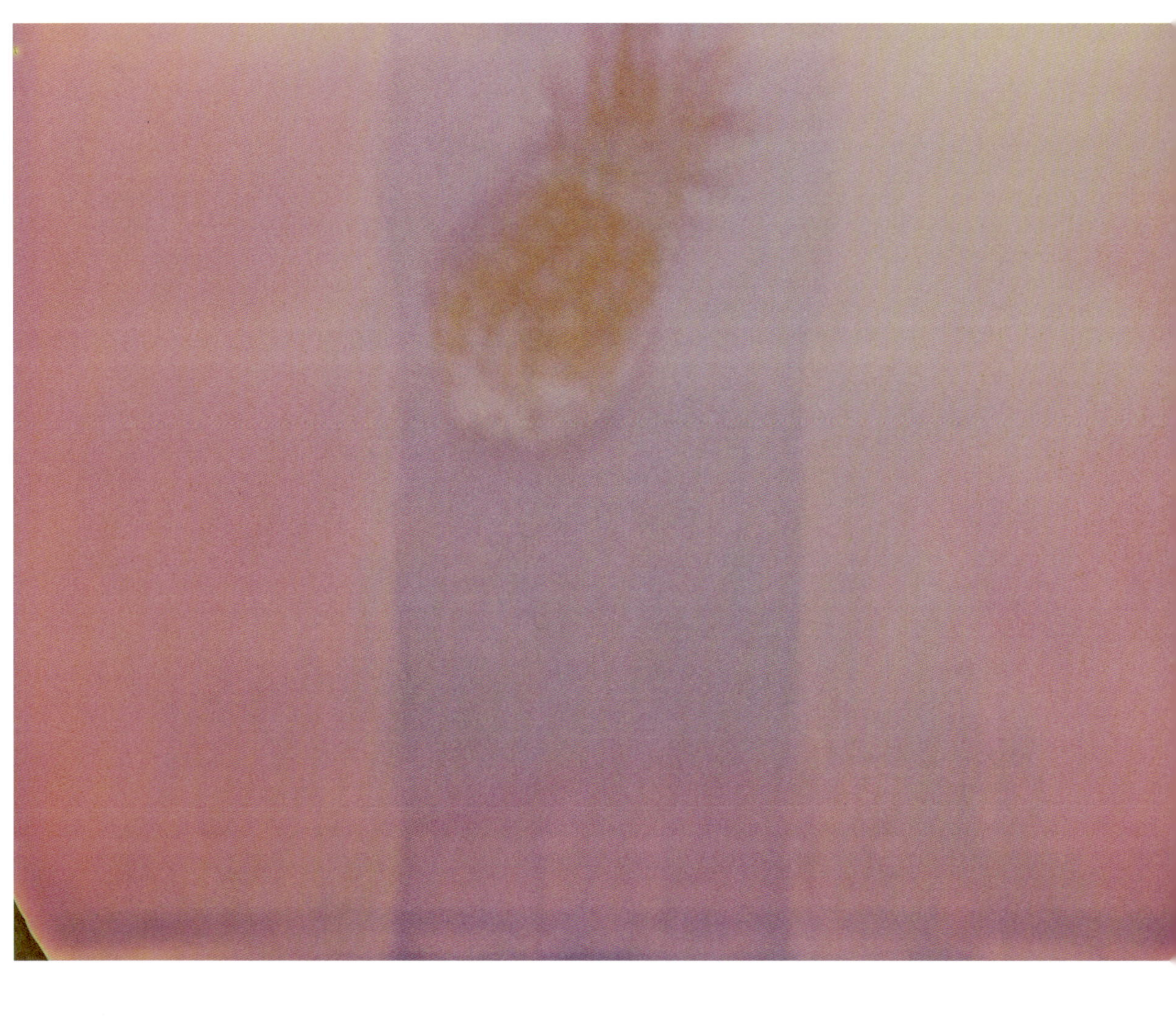

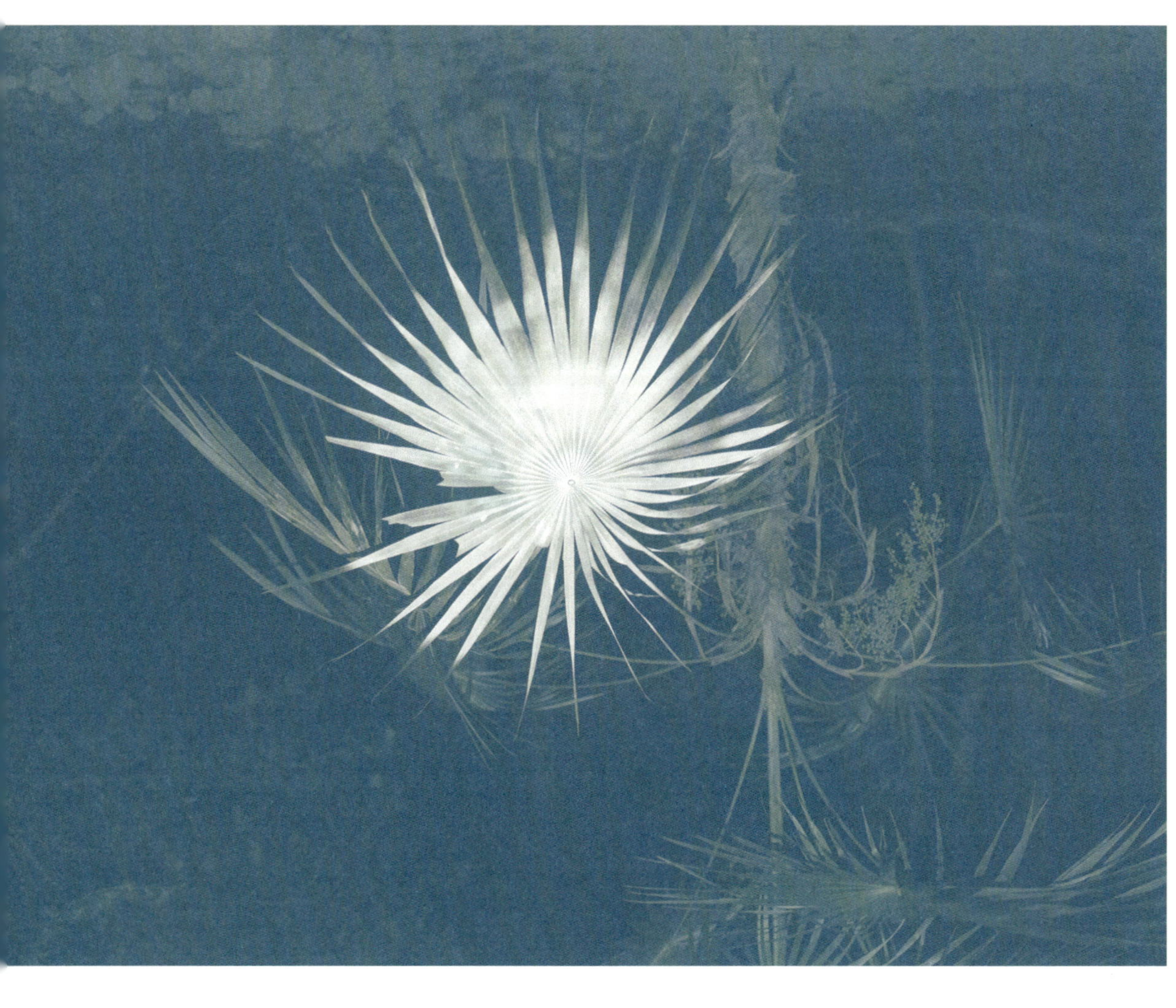

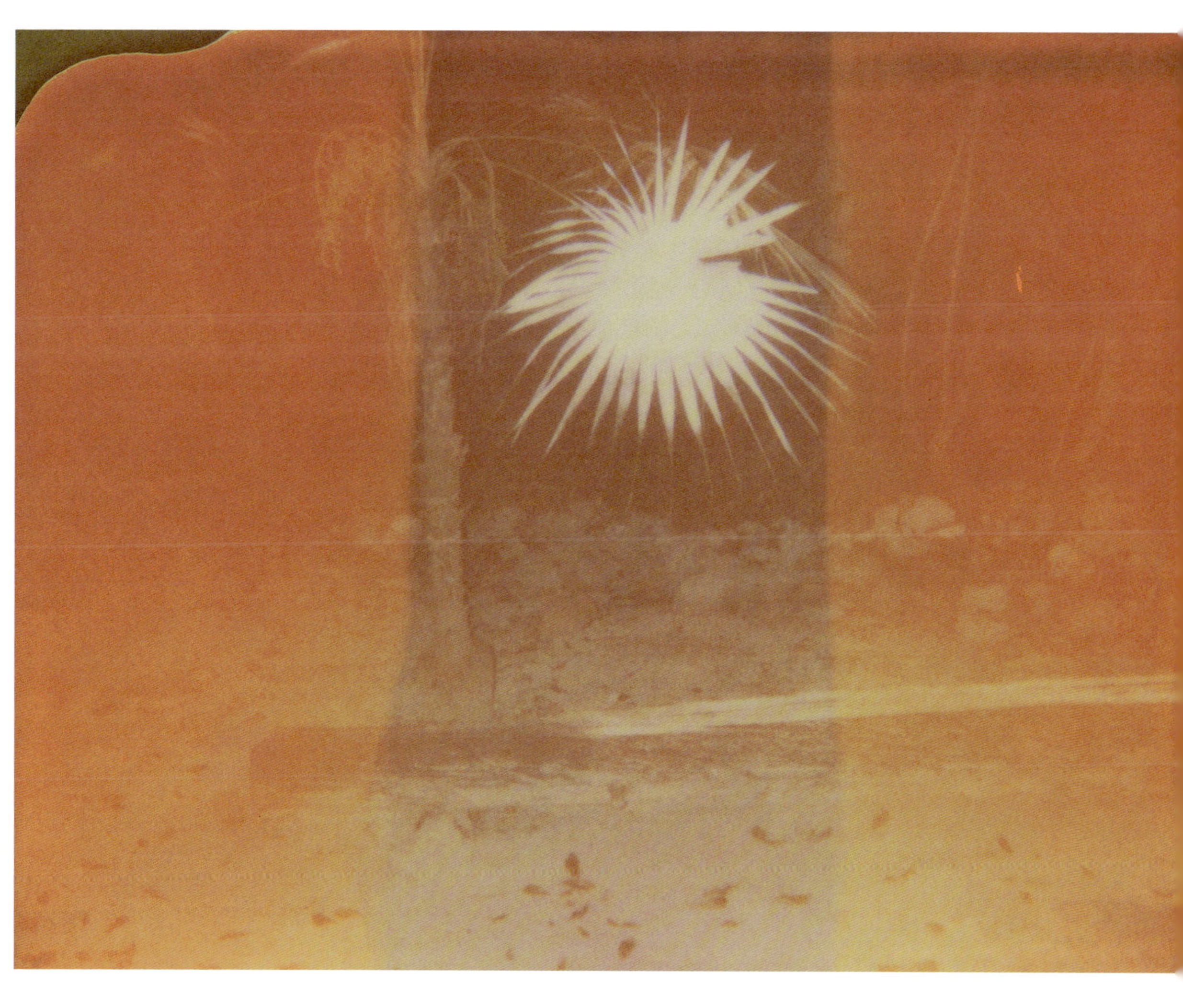

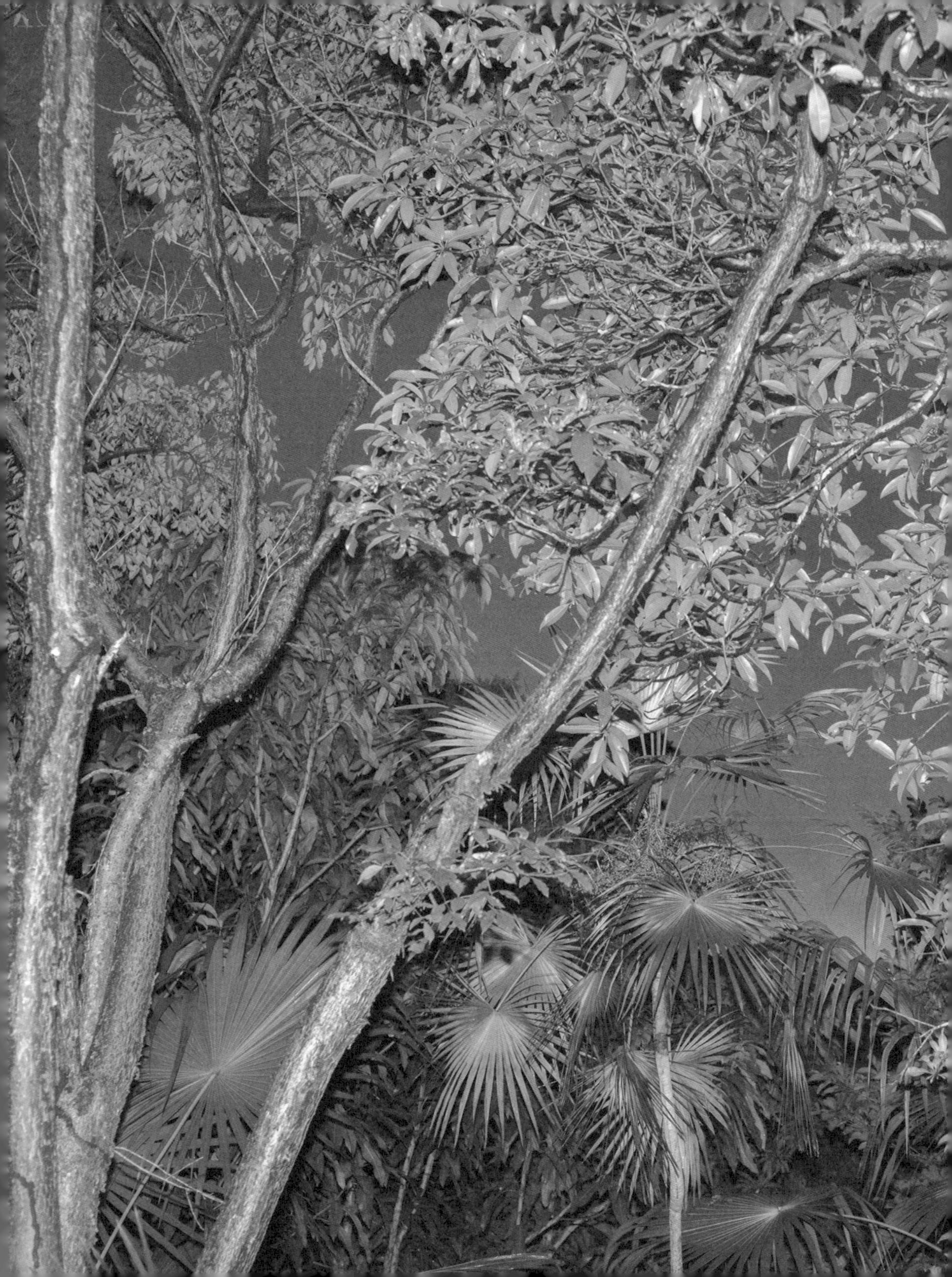

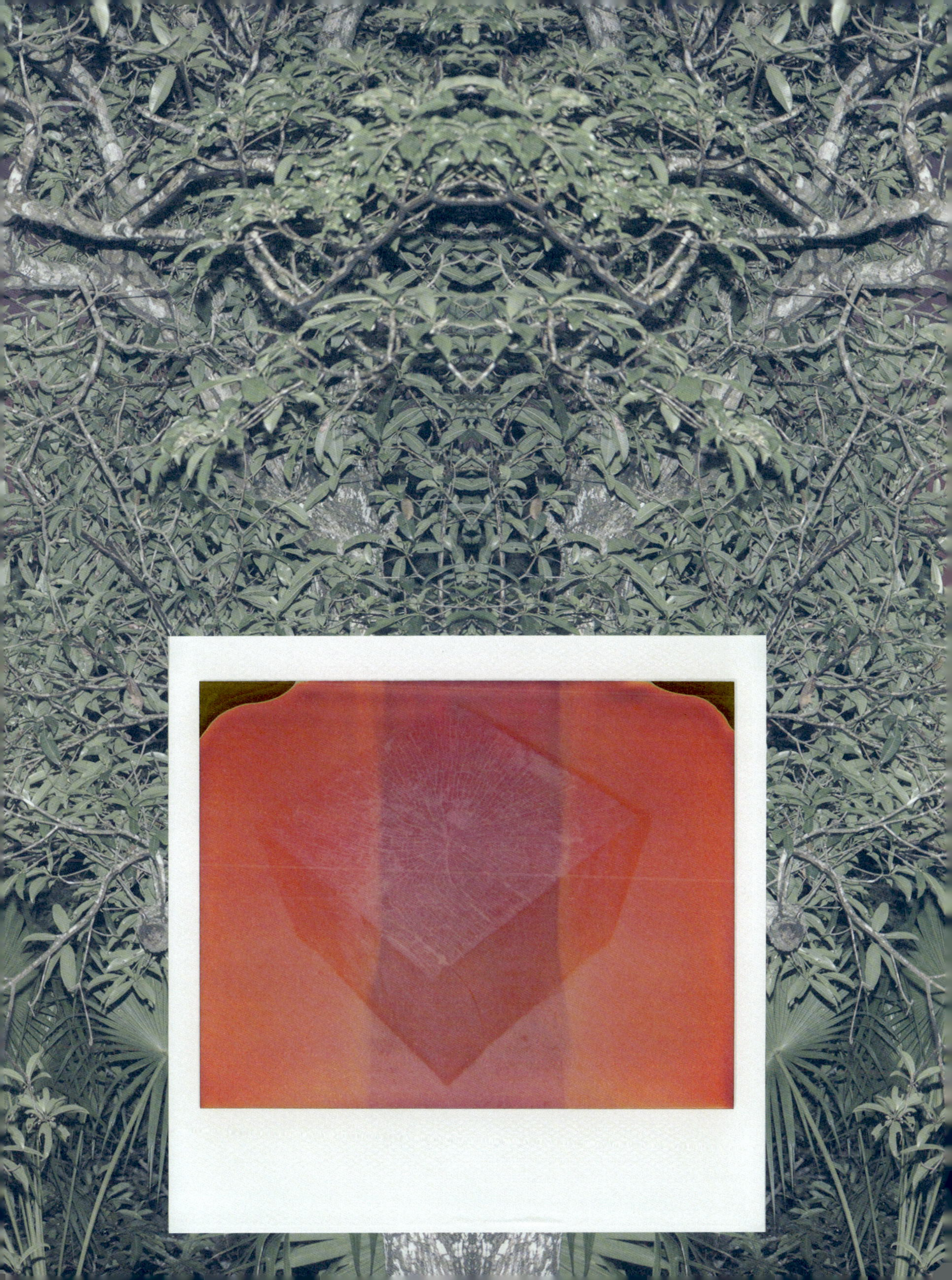

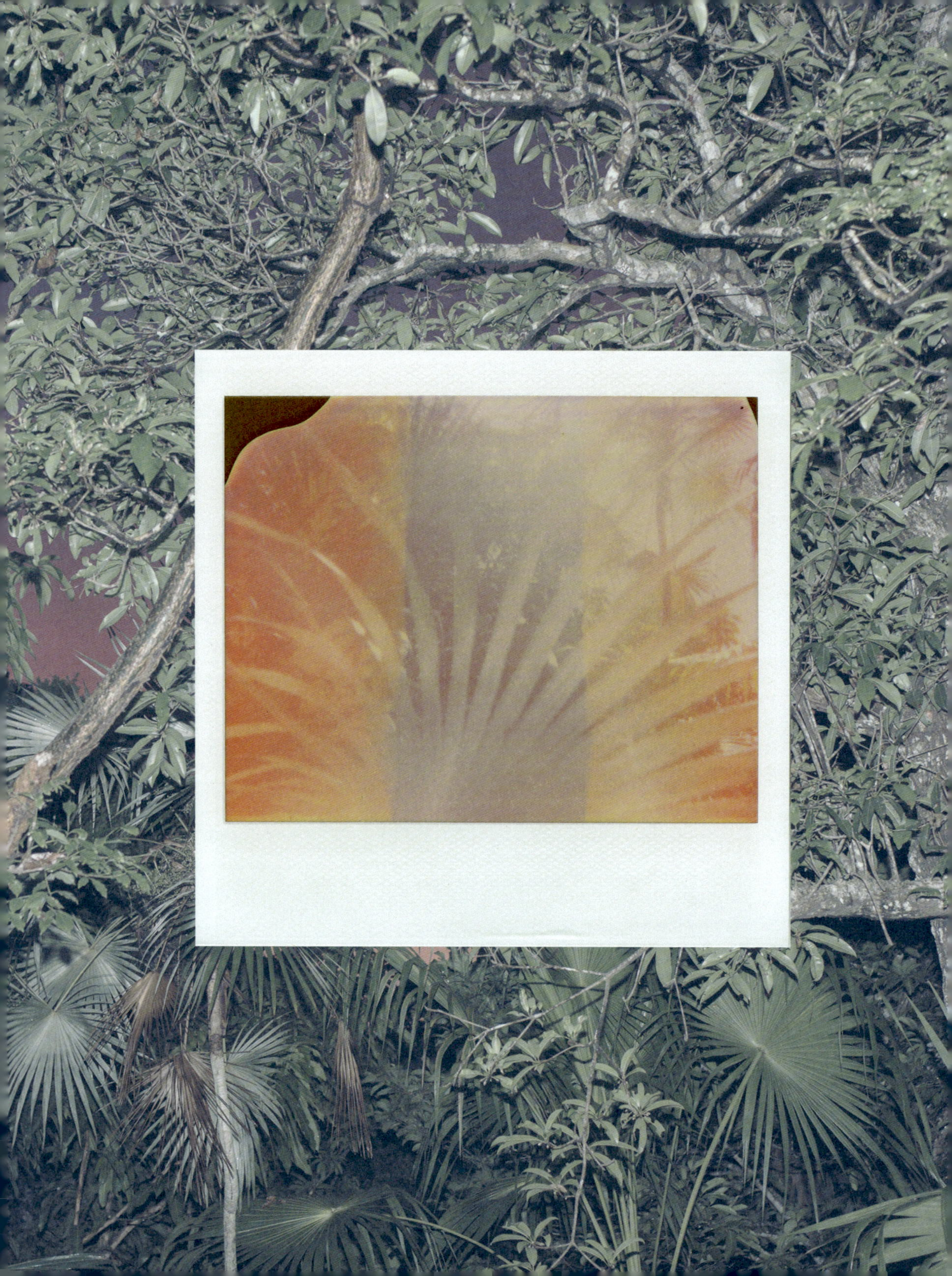

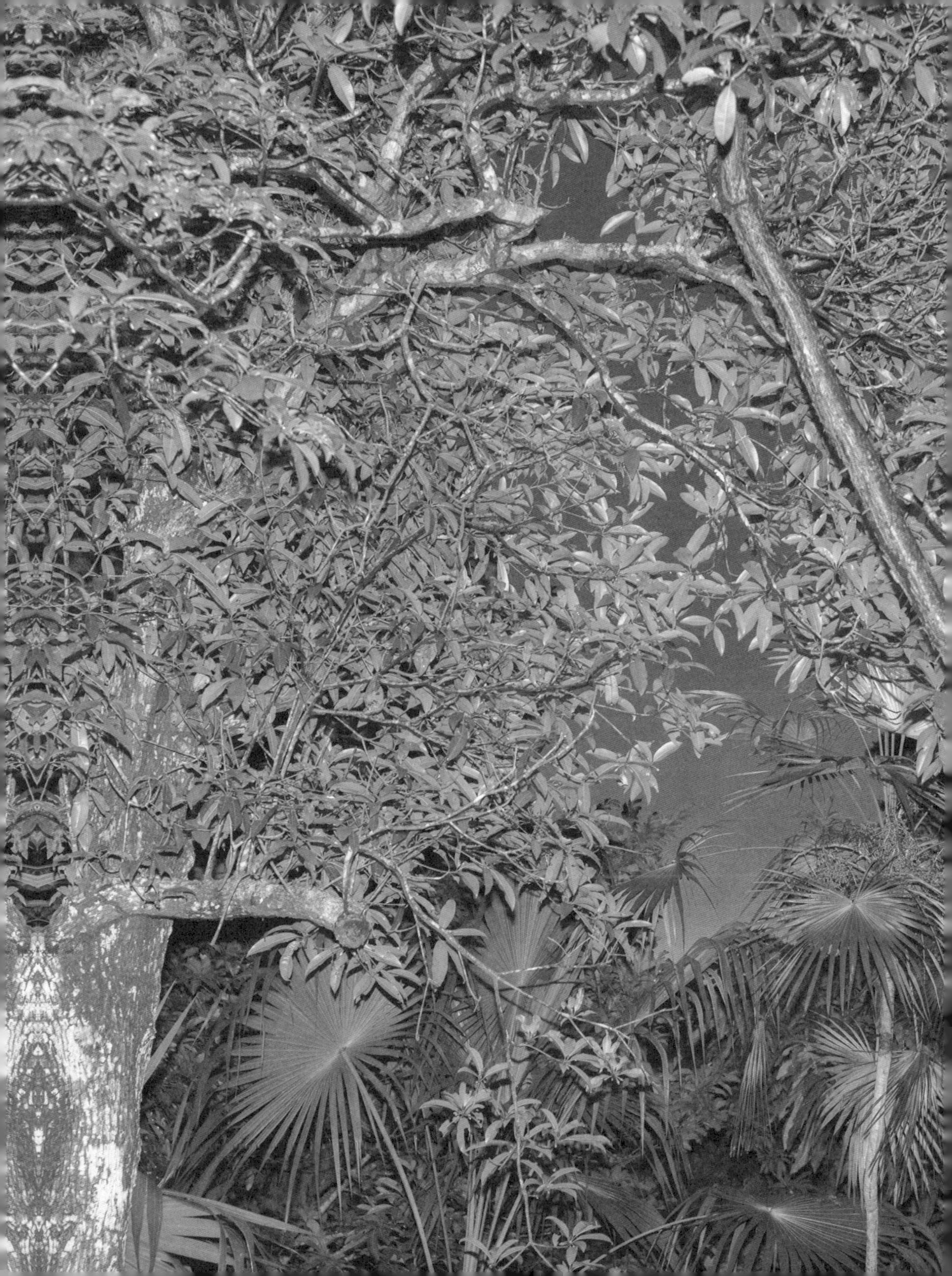

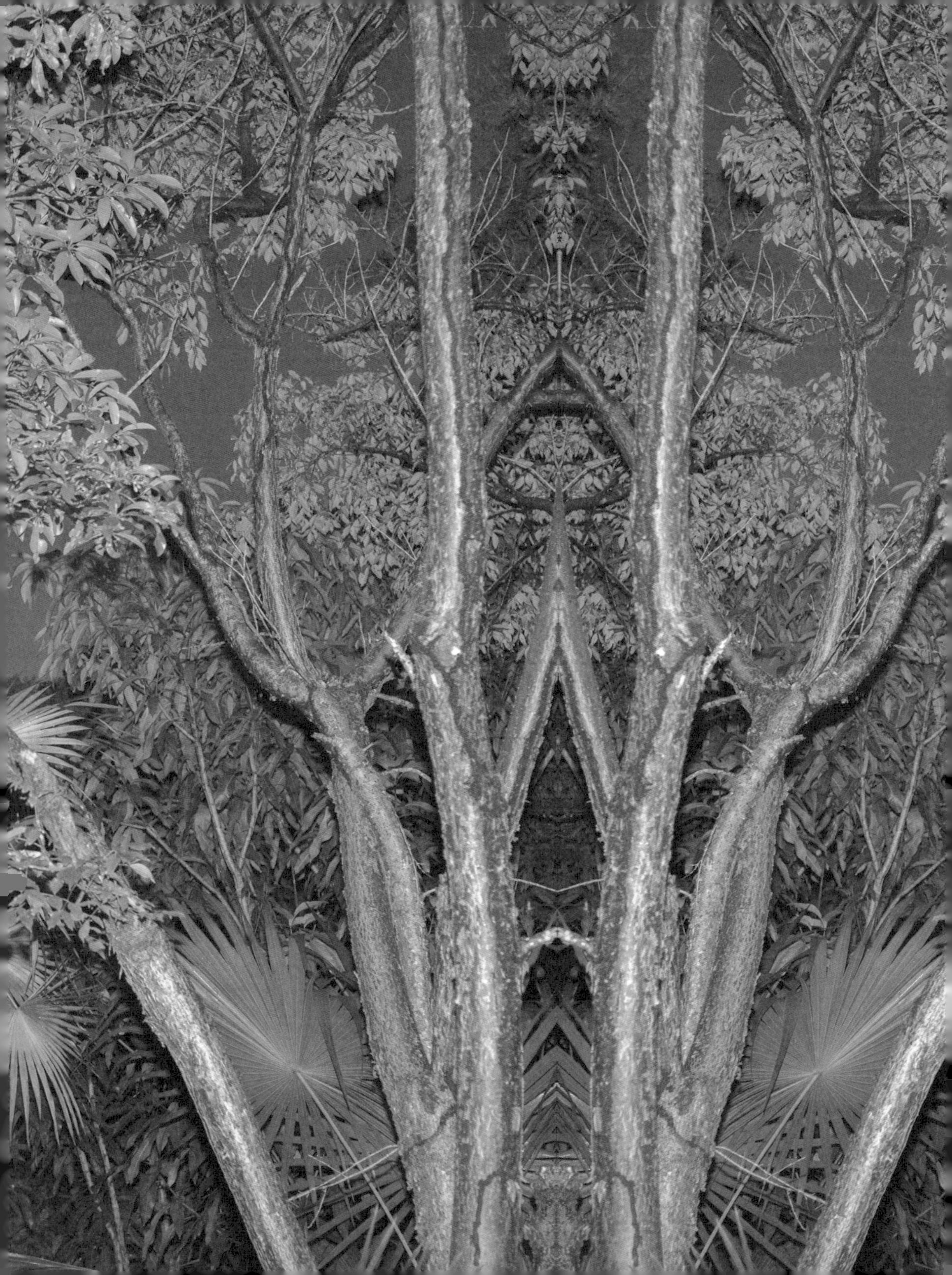

In August 2015, Cristina de Middel and Kalev Erickson reach the
Mexican peninsula of Yucatan. Alongside their camera, they also have
in their suitcases a lot of distressed Polaroid photos. Day to day, these
colour-leaking images would determine their itinerary, a journey on
the roads of oblivion. Jungle Check is the story of these two still-image
adventurers, who sought to trace and reinterpret the remains of a diffuse
past. With their golden stains, the Polaroid shots all show the same pink-
orange hue, the faded colours typical of old snaps.

Beyond their alterations, the images reveal vaguely identifiable forms:
traces of foliage or of some big cat, a dead fish or bits of some old ruins,
presumably Tulum. And it is precisely in the vicinity of the Mayan
archaeological site of Tulum that the Jungle Check adventure begins.
De Middel and Erickson thus follow in the footsteps of many an
archaeologist and adventurer attracted like them to these ancestral ruins.
Their investigation takes the form of a photographic exploration whose
premises go back to the origins of the medium itself: the photographic
reconstruction.

Right from the beginning, photography has been invested with the concept of re-photographing. The process of photographing the same phenomenon or the same landscape or the same face "before and after", will have applications in disciplines as varied as architecture, medicine, engineering, mountain conservation, forensic research or even the study of landscape. This time-tracking tool allows the comparison between two or more states or occurrences recorded by scientists, so they can study slow or quick evolutionary phenomena.

However, in the case of Jungle Check, this photographic reconstruction protocol is diverted, and finally shatters. In the first place, the objects forming the basis of the quest come from the realm of the unknown, not only because their reference images are without context and are often fuzzy, or have even disappeared, but also because this quest is situated exactly at the crossroad between the forms represented and the medium itself, a medium victim of the assault of time and the environment. During this jungle trip, the Polaroids generated new images, of which they, in some way, became the matrices. And these new images are themselves endowed with their memory.

Here a dialogue between the images is established, there the images
complement each other and seem to interlock, and elsewhere it is the
intention of the anonymous author that is brought back to life. Further
on, the new image updates the content of the old ones or borrows a
shape or a hue.

The exuberant jungle overflows. Trees and branches weave stories,
shape faces, hands and boundless landscapes. Stems split and become
the legs of some giant insects. Ruins of the past resonate with the bricks
of an abandoned construction site. A subterranean concretion from
the depth of the Earth echoes the blind and golden zones created by
the worn out Polaroid chemistry. The caves, called "cenotes", were
considered by the Mayas as direct communication channels with the gods
dwelling in the heart of the Earth. Rock is now sand and stones are blue.
A huge animal retraces its furrows while tyres etch a path in the sand.
A tiger head floats, lost in the waves of faded tints the altered chemistry
created on the paper. The triumphant and sublime flower lends its
colours to sheets of gelatine, while the grey lizard dreams of a past the

colour of fire. "The path is made by walking" it is said, but here the road sign shows nothing but its own flatness. There is no before and no after anymore, the jungle has reclaimed the land in an enchanting profusion in which mangrove and coral reefs, terrestrial mammals and reptiles, beach towels, the turquoise blue of the Caribbean sea, an unseen diver and the dazzling white beaches of fine sands that borders the jungle of Tulum coexist and intermingle.

Making two different temporalities meet and blend should only be possible with a time-machine. Invented at the end of the 19th century, the lenticular process was aimed at restoring relief. Jungle Check diverts this fantasy by overlapping and joining an image from yesterday with another from today, thus combining past and present, memory and forgetting.

Luce Lebart

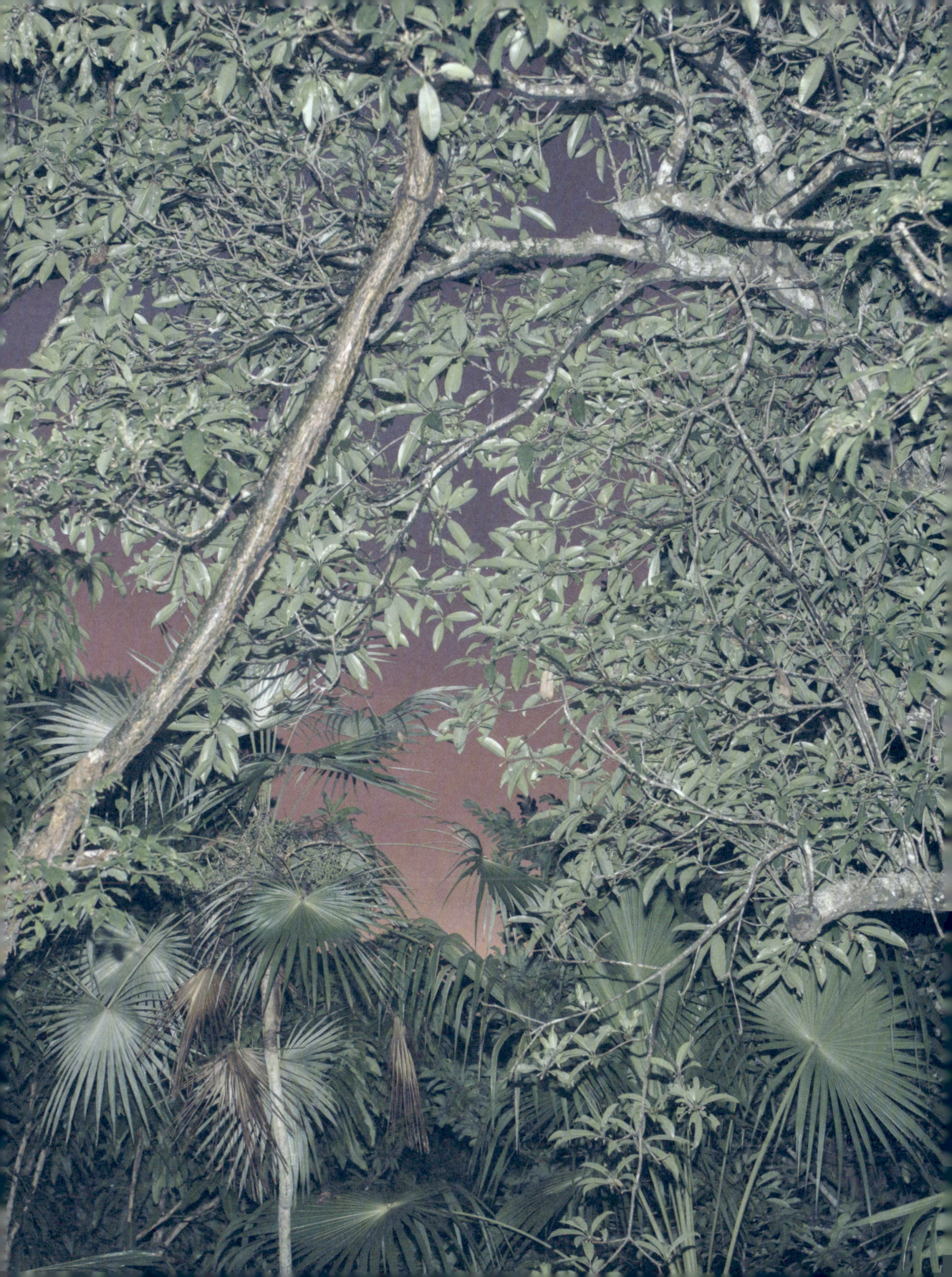

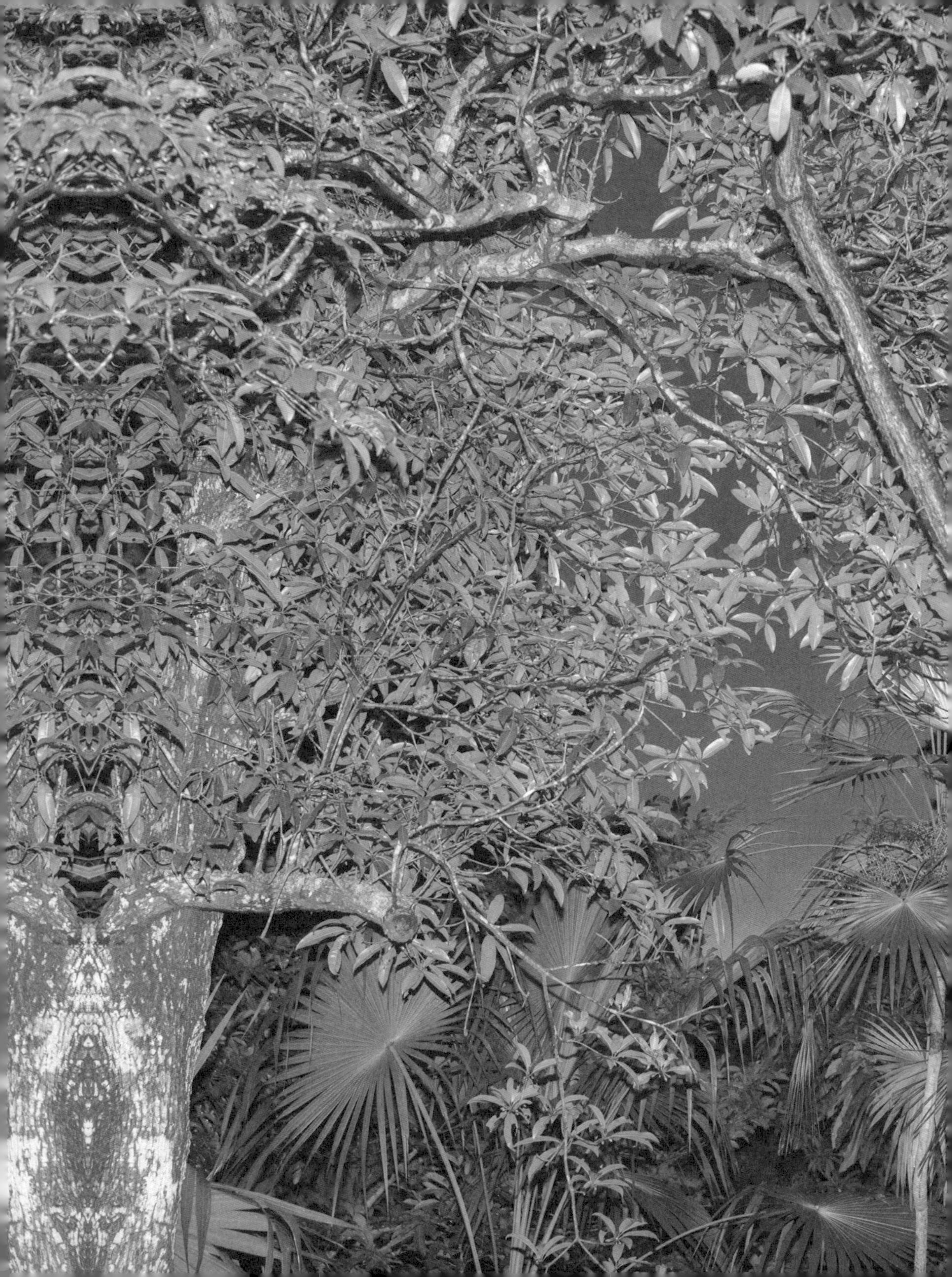

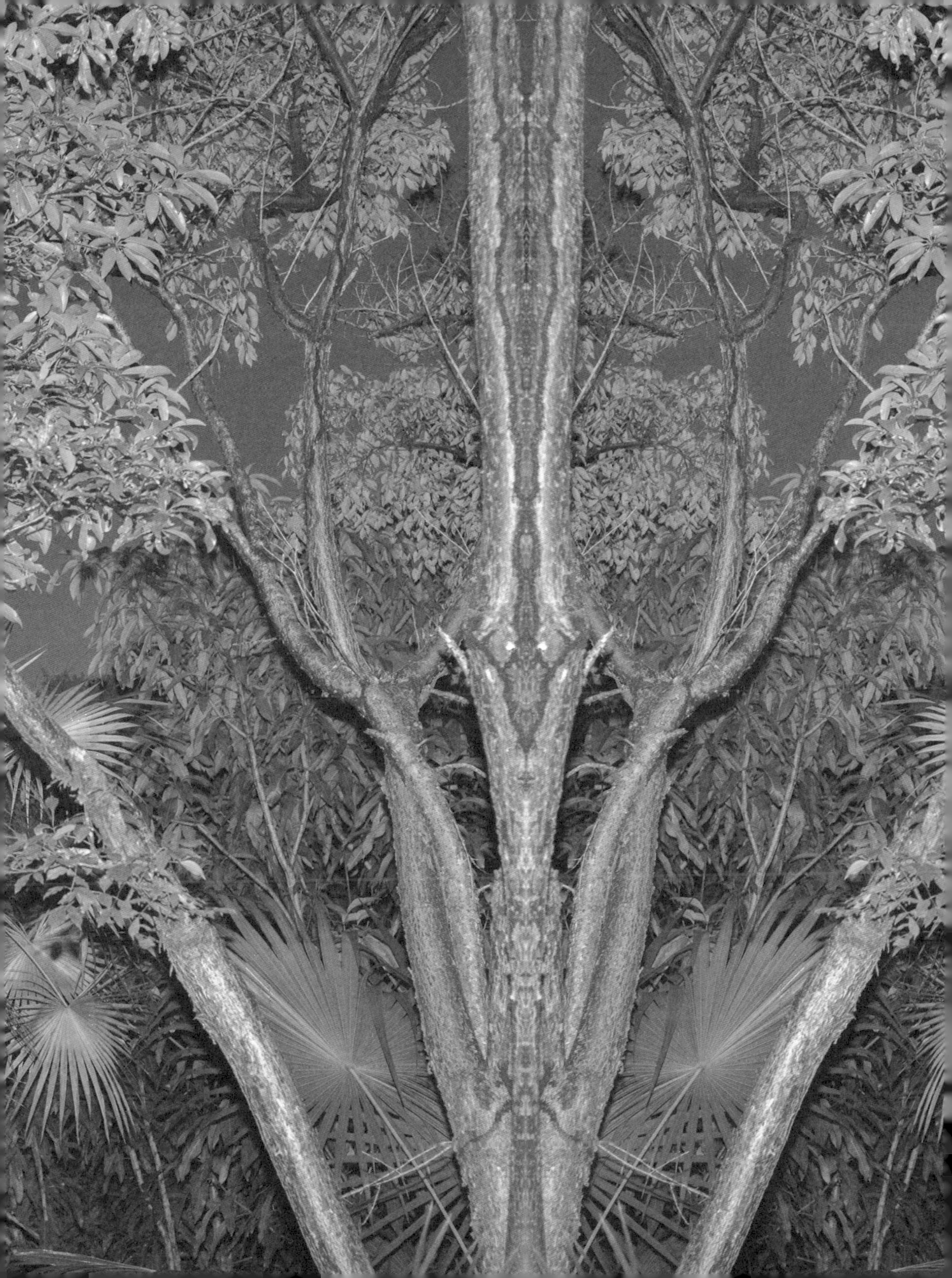

Book concept, content and design: Kalev Erickson and Cristina De Middel
Text: Luce Lebart
Translation: Christophe Dillinger
Design and production: James Welch

We would like to thank Foam for their unconditional support during the première of the series in les Rencontres d´Arles 2017 and for believing in this project from the beginning. Also, special thanks to all the insects we met in the jungle, specially the carnivore ants and the baby scorpions, for keeping us aware and ready to run throughout this adventure.

This was published with the support of the visual arts Festival Images Vevey (Switzerland) where the exhibition JUNGLE CHECK was exhibited in September 2018.

RM
© 2018
RM Verlag, S.L.
Loreto 13-15, local B
08029, Barcelona
Spain

© 2018
Editorial RM, S.A. de C.V.
Córdoba 234, int.5-6, Colonia Roma Norte
06700, Mexico City
Mexico

info@editorialrm.com
www.editorialrm.com

ISBN 978-84-17047-71-9
DL B 21566-2018

364

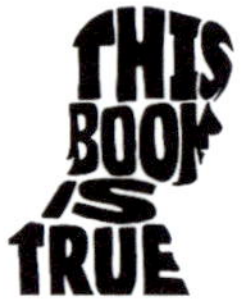

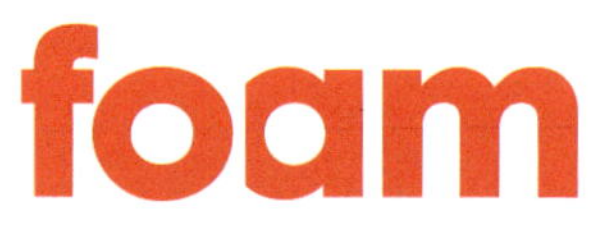